THE PRINCE OF DARKNESS

Professor Ted Wragg
Exeter University

Trentham Books
in association with *TES – Times Educational Supplement*

First published in 1998 by Trentham Books Limited

Trentham Books Limited
Westview House
734 London Road
Oakhill
Stoke on Trent
Staffordshire
England ST4 5NP

British Cataloguing in Publication Data
A catalogue record for this book is available from the
British Library
ISBN 1 85856 165 5

Cover cartoon by Jon Hall.

Designed and typeset by Trentham Print Design Ltd., Chester
and printed in Great Britain by The Cromwell Press Ltd.,
Wiltshire.

Contents

Foreword   v

Chapter 1: Don't ring us, we'll ring you
Harry the axeman, you're in detention   1
Don't you just love Melaniflips?   4
Those long balls that turn into own-goals   7
People skills for quick decision making   10
Buffeted by perils on the seas   13
Read all about the lost register drama   16
Nostalgia for the 'bad old days'   19
Uncle Ted's special stocking fillers   22
Comic relief as darkness descends   25
Awake, sleeping beauties of jargon   28
Get out before they rewrite the plot   31
The very model of a sergeant-major general   34
Fairy tales for the Loonytune league   37
Feathers ruffled by birdbrains   40
Is there an inspector in the house   43
Head feels curse of the Scottish play   46
How to kill imagination in one fell swoop   49
Jockstraps, Star Wars and vodka   52
Learn a lesson from Blackburn Rovers   56

Chapter 2: Wring out the old
Yippee! They're out, but the challenge is on   59
Cars and shades as the language of lifestyle   62
Success to the Woodlouse initiative   65
Economical with the classroom actualité   68
Digits that add up to a plethora of piffle   71
Conference call from the cowshed   74
For Alan Shearer, read Tinky Winky   77

Warning: Literacy can damage relationships with
your children   80
Too hot to trot in the discipline dance   83
Problems solved at the drop of a hat   86
Recruitment needs more than sweeteners   89
Come on down, Joe Targeteer   92
Spicy Chris and Mel on a unicycle   95
Who shall punish the punishers?   98
Hitlists, gremlins and a new song   101
Calculators may be used off the bone   104

Chapter 3: Ring in the New?
What's that in newspeak?   107
Funny business this profit motive   110
Carry on busking   113
Titans' clash forces debate into corners   116
Give norm-crushers their head   119
The bogeyman who won't shut up   122
Love is a nod, a grunt and your own chair   125
A mantra does not a lesson make   128
Seize the day ... and the money   131
Please don't beam me over   134
And for our next trick ...   137
Dalek dogma is a bitter pill   140
Could do better ...   143
Wallop the teacher, 50p a go   146
Bite your nails? That's nothing   149
Are you listening, bankers?   152
How to tackle the little sods   154
Teacher watch: a summer special   157

Foreword

Why Prince of Darkness? Well, back in February 1998, Chris Woodhead, Chief Inspector of Schools, attracted yet another headline when he attacked those who were supposedly at the 'heart of darkness' in education. As an educator devising new curricula, directing major research projects, teaching not only in my own university, but also in primary and secondary schools, I had always seen myself as being at the heart of daylight, but there I was, named alongside some of the most distinguished professors of education in the land. It could have been worse. Woodhead could have spoken of me with approval, thereby ruining my professional street credibility completely.

So I wrote a piece in the *Times Educational Supplement*, included in this book, entitled *The bogeyman who won't shut up*. In it I described how I would be filling out Woodhead's 'Victorian demon' fantasy by putting on my Prince of Darkness outfit and leaping out suddenly on him, crying, 'Look out! There's a professor of education on the loose. Run for your life. Here comes the bogeyman. Whooooooooo!!'

Over the years various people have tried to shut me up. Under the Conservatives, well meaning senior civil servants used to take me on one side to tell me that, if only I said nice things about ministers, untold honours and bounties might come my way. I was 'leaned on' as well, sometimes cleverly, sometimes not so subtly. None of it made the slightest bit of difference. As an academic in everyday life I don't actually care whether I offend the powerful. I am just grateful that academics still have an opportunity to speak out, while others are gagged. Satire is mostly driven by anger. Humour is just the vehicle.

The Prince of Darkness is the ninth published collection of my satirical essays. It covers the two year period, from September 1996 to July 1998, when the Conservatives finally lost power and a new Labour government took over. In this collection the essays appear in chronological order, so the first chapter goes up to the general election in May 1997, while chapters 2 and 3 chronicle respectively the rest of 1997 and the first few months of 1998 under the incoming Labour administration.

Ted Wragg

Chapter 1
Don't ring us, we'll ring you

Harry the axeman, you're in detention

Anyone who spent a fortune on the Mediterranean seeking a little relaxation in the sun could have saved the money and enjoyed the usual Summer seaside variety show in the comfort of their own armchair.

Not for nothing is August known as the 'silly season'. If you want to witness announcements the Government would rather you missed, or spectate at one of the many free end-of-pier reviews, then sit patiently at home and wait for the annual film show.

It was all there once more. As the sun shone, out came the comedians in baggy trousers and the clowns, right on cue: 'The exam pass rates have gone up. End of civilisation as we know it. We'll all be murdered in our beds'.

This year, we were told, the Government decided to tell the critics of higher exam pass rates to shut up. I am sure it had nothing at all to do with the nearness of a general election and the need to suggest that all is well in education, or to win a few friends.

One Government official was quoted as saying: 'It is about time these doom and gloom merchants shut up and recognised the achievement of the candidates and of the parents and teachers who have supported them. This is the culmination of two years of hard work and we should be celebrating the better results, not whingeing'.

Precisely. So why has the very same Government spent the last few years moaning each Summer about falling standards and setting up rigorous and far-reaching enquiries?

Another piece of high comedy occurred in the middle of August, when many people had gratefully fled to Skegness or Benidorm. There was an announcement that would have been greeted with utter incredulity in any other decade since the

1

beginning of time. Instead it was met with indifference.

The news that the contract for administering nursery school and playgroup inspections had been awarded to Group 4, a security company which had hitherto specialised in the guarding of buildings and escorting prisoners, should have taken people's breath away.

In the end it was actually a relief. It could have been much worse. In these mad and desperate times, the Government might easily have given the contract to a row of motorway cones, the traffic lights on Blackpool sea front, or to the laughing hyenas at London Zoo.

Group 4 will not actually carry out the inspections themselves, but will be responsible for the administration of them. So what might the future hold?

Will two burly blokes in black leathers and crash helmets hustle inspection teams with blankets over their heads in and out of Little Piddlington Nursery? Might some Registered Inspector, while inspecting Lower Swinesville Playgroup, make an excuse to go to the toilet, and then climb out of the back window and leg it into the dusk?

It seems not to matter nowadays whether or not an individual or commercial outfit has any experience or expertise in education. The whole enterprise is up for grabs. Infant school teaching can be done by John Major's hapless 'Mums' Army', and the inspection of schools, according to the late great Kenneth Clarke, may be carried out by anybody, even a butcher. Goodbye educational expertise and specialist knowledge.

Is it unnecessarily narrow-minded and priggish to insist on the value of relevant professional knowledge in education? After all, we don't hear of doctors moaning about refuse collectors being allowed to do transplant surgery, or lawyers complaining that lucrative prosecution and defence briefs are going to night-club bouncers. Perhaps it hasn't been suggested yet.

Maybe the whole of education should just be opened up completely to commercial bidders. The 2nd Paras could all become deputy heads responsible for pupil discipline. Any school claiming its governing body is moribund could call in the Incorporated Association of Mortuary Attendants. The Fraud Squad might collect all the information for league tables.

Geography could be taught by the Automobile Association. They must have been called out to most places in their time. Maths might be covered by Camelot and be based entirely on the probability and statistics of running the national lottery. Estate agents could teach English, especially the bit about familiarity with myths and legends.

In these market-mad times, however, it is only fair that if other agencies can get involved in education, teachers should be allowed to have contracts in other fields too. Indeed, if Group 4 can administer school inspections, why cannot teachers look after the security of buildings and escort prisoners?

Useful extra cash could be earned by teachers sitting in office blocks and banks each night, playing bridge and trying not to catch the head's eye when someone is needed to patrol the corridors. Escorting prisoners would be a doddle.

'Right everybody, pay attention. Look, Harry the Axeman, that's the last time I tell you. Put that hatchet down now, and get back into line. Any more of that and you'll miss playtime. Right. I'm going to call the register. Strangler?'

'Absent, sir'.

'Embezzler?'.

'On work experience'.

'Pickpocket? Has anyone seen Pickpocket. Look, settle down, everybody. All right, all right. Who's taken my wallet? Come on, own up. I'm not going on until somebody owns up'.

'It weren't us, sir'.

'Right, have it your way. It's your time you're wasting. I'm just going to sit here, I've got plenty of books to mark. You're not going to Pentonville until somebody owns up'.

Specialist knowledge? Who needs it?

6 September 1996

Don't you just love Melaniflips?

From time to time I read a book, an article, or a text of one kind or another, that has me reaching for the Rennies. It doesn't happen often, as I am one of those tolerant chaps, more than willing to switch off the crap detector in the interests of broadening my mind.

Like many other readers of the *Observer*, I waded through two whole pages summarising the book *All Must Have Prizes* by that newspaper's journalist Melanie Phillips. Since then I have read the book as well.

At first I was more than a bit upset at the sustained attack on education it contained, but before long I felt quite excited at the birth of a new genre.

For those who have never read any of Melanie Phillips's vitriol about education, here is a sample from the book: 'But the teachers' task is therefore now all but impossible, not least because their own professional culture has become subverted by the self-destructive orthodoxy of moral and cultural relativism, the doctrine that no value or activity can be held to be any better or worse than any other.'

No value or activity can be held to be any better or worse than any other? Now I don't know about you, but I have never in my life actually met one single teacher who believes anything of the sort. We have 400,000 teachers in our schools, so I wonder where these weird people are who apparently believe that murder, arson, violence, theft, torture, cannot 'be held to be any better or worse' than unselfishness, kindness, friendship, virtue, or loving care.

The 'evidence' in the book to support these kinds of assertions consists substantially of dozens of footnotes, called variously 'Conversation with author', 'Correspondence with author', or 'Author's sources'. Figures called 'political insiders' flit in and out, and there is uncritical reproduction of the views of right-wing think tanks.

The national curriculum, according to Melanie, was established by what she calls 'progressive revolutionaries'. Teachers objected to tests because they were afraid they would be seen to have failed.

Yet for the first time in our history, both people in charge of the curriculum and assessment councils were from the Number 10 policy unit. Far from being the cause of curriculum chaos, it was teachers and others working in education who predicted most of it before the national curriculum was ever introduced.

Julian Haviland, in his book *Take Care, Mr Baker!*, analysed all the responses, nearly 12,000 of them, to the 1987 national curriculum consultation document. He pointed out at the time that every single respondent, even those in favour of a national curriculum, rejected the model being proposed.

What is exciting, however, is the brand new style of book that *All Must Have Prizes* represents. The 'Melaniflips' genre offers an immense liberation. Think of a few prejudices, quote some of your mates, and you're away. I could scarcely wait to write my very own Melaniflips.

ALL MUST HAVE EARACHE
A new Melaniflips by Ted Wragg

Don't you just hate loud pop music? Like most people[1], I certainly do. It can drive you mad[2]. The vast majority of those who play pop music at a high volume are probably idiots who should be strung up[3]. I bet the next generation will be born with transistor radios welded to their ear lobes!

I've been looking into the scientific evidence on this one. My mate Alf Dubbins says he thinks it's the long hair some young people have nowadays. If your hair grows too long it bungs up your ears so you can't hear. According to Alf[4] this makes it highly likely that your ears will simply drop off and you'll need a transistor radio instead.

In fact, he's got a pal, Fred Gubbins, who swears he's actually seen a lad with a radio instead of ears, when he was on holiday in Skegness[5] last year. I've been to Skegness myself, but I've never actually seen the lad in question. But then, I can't stand Skegness ever since a job lot of bird dung landed on my new jacket[6] as I walked along the seafront.

The trouble with modern youth is they make far too much noise. They're always chattering in class when they're at school. After they leave, they get a car and everybody[7] complains like mad when they turn their car hi-fi up to maximum volume.

I would go so far as to say that the evidence against modern youth is now one hundred per cent solid[8]. The only answer is for youth to be closed down completely until they've grown up and are as sensible and as old as my friends[9] and me.

There is no doubt who is to blame for all this. It's the teachers' fault[10].

References

1   e.g. D Duck in a Disney cartoon, I forget the title now, when the three little ducks made a lot of noise and he shouted at them.
2   D Duck again, *op cit* (I think he threw something at them).
3   Conversation with taxi driver, somewhere near Charing Cross, circa April 1995.
4   Dubbins, A., in conversation with the author and a little bloke in a trilby hat, Pig and Whistle saloon bar, late 1995 or early 1996.
5   Gubbins, F., postcard to Dubbins, A., from Skegness, August 1995.
6   Communication with seagull, July 1991.
7   My dad, most days from 1956 to 1989.
8   Author's sauce, 1996.
9   Dubbins, A. and Gubbins, F. again.
10   Phillips, Melanie (1996) *All Must Have Prizes*, almost any page.

20 September 1996

Those long balls that turn into own-goals

English football was ruined for over a decade by what became known as the 'long ball game'. For those who are not familiar with football tactics, and indeed who are wondering what on earth there is in common between education and kicking a bag of wind, now that Kenneth Clarke has moved on, let me explain.

The 'long ball game' was the nearest equivalent that football had to a national curriculum. It was not compulsory, but virtually everybody played it, as it was the principal orthodoxy peddled on official football coaching courses.

The 'strategy', for want of a better word, consisted of muscular defenders picking up the ball in their own half, hoofing it miles into the air, hoping frantically it would land on the head of one of their forwards. Meanwhile the delicate dwarfs who played in attacking positions waited patiently at the other end of the pitch, about seventy yards away. It was like carthorses lobbing chainsaws to surgeons.

More often than not a gigantic defender of the opposing side would say 'Thank you very much', flatten the poor midget attacker who was making a frantic attempt to leap more than three inches off the ground, and hoist the ball seventy yards into the stratosphere on its way back to the very player who had propelled it to him in the first place.

This crude aerial ping pong led to English teams being regularly annihilated by those foreign teams who did not actually die laughing at the unsubtle and brain-corroding nature of it all. English football is only just shaking itself loose from this dour stranglehold.

The link between our recent national football tactics and education is simple. We are now being told by Chris Woodhead that the findings of inspection reports will be translated into a prescribed national curriculum for the training of novice and experienced teachers. The long ball game in football was based on a similar assumption.

Some quite careful analysis of football league matches had shown that there was often a 'long ball' in the five moves leading up to the scoring of a goal. I suspect there were also lots of other frequently occurring events, like someone spitting on the floor, or breaking wind, but I digress.

The assumption was made that it was the seventy yard hoick that must have 'caused' the goal. Therefore, simple conclusion: if everybody does it, they will all score goals.

So did matches end up with one team winning by ten goals to nine? No, not really. In the event there were lots of extremely boring 0 – 0 draws. Opposing teams neutralised each other because the element of surprise had disappeared. What is worse, many of our footballers lost not only their inventiveness, but also their repertoire of craft skills.

It would be nice to think that school inspection reports could be neatly translated into what Chris Woodhead referred to as 'absolutes' at a conference at which we both spoke. Unfortunately the research into teacher effectiveness, both in Britain and the United States, has never come up with any blanket prescriptions that could remotely be referred to as 'absolutes' without stretching the meaning of the word well beyond breaking point.

Is it better, for example, to ask children more of what some people call 'higher order questions', that is, questions requiring a reply that goes beyond the mere recall of information? Two American researchers, both of whom had analysed several research studies of teachers' questions and pupil learning, came to opposite conclusions. One decided it was, the other that it wasn't.

There was a well-intended attempt in the United States to draw up a set of 'Teacher should....' statements. They consisted of assertions like 'During reading-group instruction, teachers should give a maximal amount of brief feedback and provide fast-paced activities of the 'drill' type'. However, these were voluntary for teachers, not prescribed by the Government.

Is Chris Woodhead right? Can inspection reports be turned into prescribed teaching styles? Or is this just an example of him living up to the poignant bathos of his surname? My experience of inspection reports and research findings is that it is not that simple.

The context of teaching is vital – the age, background and prior knowledge of the children, the subject or topics being taught, the time, space and materials available, the personality and expertise of the teacher. Teachers need to be able to make dozens of judicious on-the-spot decisions about what makes best sense, not consult an official omni-purpose Government handbook.

Research tends to produce general areas of interest, but with great variation in individual interpretation. For example, in the research project I am currently directing we found, among other things, that teachers whose pupils improved most in reading made literacy important, maximised the time children spent on their task, and individualised their teaching. But they often did it in quite different ways.

The Teacher Training Agency was quoted as saying that you wouldn't want doctors to say they used 'a variety of methods'. Yes you would. And you certainly wouldn't want the Government telling doctors what to do.

For years the bog standard National Health Service operation for varicose veins in the leg consisted of a series of horizontal incisions which left livid scars about an inch or more long. A surgeon I know has a better technique. He makes tiny vertical incisions which eventually leave a small number of virtually invisible white dots, much neater, though more expensive, than the 'official' version.

So will the Woodhead plan go ahead? Will he of the ligneous noddle create the pedagogical equivalent of the long ball in football?

I hope simple-minded prescriptions are not introduced, but, like English football players, I wouldn't be too surprised to see a lot of balls coming from on high.

4 October 1996

People skills for quick decision making

Have you ever worked out how many decisions you make in a single day? The answer, if you are a teacher, is probably well over a thousand. In fact, if anyone ever offers you a job at piecework rates, £1 per decision, knock them over and sign the contract before they change their mind. You will retire shortly on the proceeds.

Many teachers engage in 100 to 200 transactions in an hour. During rapid fire oral questioning they may ask 50 questions within ten or a dozen minutes. For each decision numerous factors have to be taken into account – the age and background of the pupils, the subject matter, the previous history of the class, the purposes of the activity.

Yet many decisions are made in a second or less. It is astonishing how much information the human brain can process. When Jack Kerr, who used to be professor of science education at Leicester University, had retired, he once told me that the biggest change was the disappearance of rapid decision making. All he had to decide each day was whether to go to Tesco in the morning and the library in the afternoon, or the other way round.

I love American books on teachers' decision making. They sometimes depict a bizarre world. One such book, by Dale Brubaker and Lawrence Simon, is subtitled 'Real-life cases to hone your people skills'. I've been carefully honing my people skills ever since I read the case studies in it.

'A student bursts into your class first thing in the morning and says that a small group of boys is excitedly milling around a wastebasket in the restroom. The wastebasket has a gun in it. What will you do?'

Well it does make a change from throwing a fit about chewing gum in the wastebasket. The authors' favoured response is

'Contact the principal immediately and have the principal deal with the matter'. So 'dump it on someone who earns more' is the message. One frightening American statistic is that 100,000 American pupils may carry a gun, and 160,000 play truant every day through fear of sustaining physical injury.

Another decision problem reads: 'You are a teacher, and it comes to your attention that the teacher in the next room to you is making negative comments to students, the principal, other teachers, and parents regarding your teaching. What will you do?'

The authors' favoured response this time is 'Ignore the colleague's comments and go about your business, continuing to use your present approach to teaching'. I would have preferred: 'Race round to your colleague and deliver a right upper-cut, while saying, 'Try honing your people skills on this, sun-shine'', but it did not figure amongst the options.

It is all too easy to disagree with someone else's solutions, but I did feel uneasy at some of the proposed decisions. In one scene the city orchestra is performing during assembly, when four or five boys in the balcony decide to chatter noisily and drop their books.

'Take this matter to the faculty advisory council', is the recommended response. The faculty advisory council may not meet till a week on Tuesday. The answer 'go over and deal with it' is rejected, as it would be intrusive and call attention to yourself. But then, so would a negligence suit if the books land on somebody's head.

This multiple choice approach to decision making could be an exciting part of the new national curriculum for the in-service training of experienced teachers (old lags' badge), with the Government-favoured responses gaining full marks and a merit award, and the 'wish fulfilment' answers getting five added pension years and early retirement. Hone your people skills on these three.

The head arrives at school rolling drunk. Which do you say?

(a) 'You should be ashamed of yourself, I'm reporting you to the governors'

(b) 'You should be ashamed of yourshelf, sho get your handsh off my vodka bottle'.

At a parents' evening a father accuses you of not giving his son high enough marks. Which response would you give?

(a) 'I apologise most profusely. Under the conditions of the parent's charter I am more than happy to revise the assessment'.

(b) 'Now I've met you I can see the poor little blighter is battling against the genetic odds, so I'll give him five extra marks for heroism'.

The chairman of an interviewing committee for a senior post asks you what you would bring to the school if you were appointed. How do you reply?

(a) 'A wealth of experience, a strong professional commitment, and boundless energy and enthusiasm'.

(b) 'A big chip on each shoulder, an even bigger mortgage, arthritis, and several shelves of hardly used national curriculum folders'.

18 October 1996

Buffeted by perils on the seas

It is too late now, the moment has passed, but the advertising literature for the 'Half Term Management School' offered an intriguing way of keeping heads and teachers out of mischief. Gluttons for punishment were invited to spend their half term on a course.

'You deserve a development opportunity but you can't leave your pupils during the school week', said the blurb. The solution was to go on the half term management course. It summed up one of the problems for people who work in education: they are buried under demands of one kind or another, but have little time to reflect on them.

Small wonder that so few people apply for headships nowadays. One secondary school attracted no serious applicants the first time its headship was advertised. Another vacancy, in a large secondary school in an attractive location, had received over 150 applications when it was last advertised in the mid 1980s. This year there were just 17.

The literature on school effectiveness often identifies the head teacher as a key factor in successful schools. There is another side to this coin, however. In the 'blame culture' in which we now live and work, if all is not well, then the head takes the rap. Perhaps an honest advert for the job ought to state: 'Wanted: barmy, broad-shouldered masochist. The successful candidate will be pilloried whenever fertiliser hits the fan'.

'Head teacher as football manager' is one of many roles attached to a senior post. Football managers are of several kinds. The survivors are both knowledgeable and phlegmatic, usually good at dealing with people inside and outside their organisation.

Almost all the best football managers have been sacked at some time in their career. They took the blame for circumstances that were often beyond their control, like having no money to buy decent players, or pay sufficient wages to the ones they had.

The daily pressures sometimes led them into becoming 'characters'. Brian Clough, the former Nottingham Forest manager, was regarded as irascible, but he gave considerable confidence to players who were unsure of themselves, while reprimanding those who thought they knew it all. 'Differentiation' is not just something that happens in teaching.

Pressures on head teachers to come top of the performance leagues have brought the football manager analogy closer. I met a teacher who complained that her school had had four heads in as many years, well up to football manager standards.

One of the four had simply announced that she would not be coming into school the following Monday. This is known as the 'Auf Wiedersehen' solution. In this case 'Auf Wiedersehen' means 'I'll be seeing you – but not in school'.

There are many other roles that head teachers play. One is that of karaoke singer. If you have ever tried the noble art of karaoke singing, you will know that the pre-recorded music ploughs remorselessly on, even if you lose your place, choke on the high notes, or collapse with mirth at the lyrics. Headship can be like singing to a karaoke machine, chasing an unstoppable, externally set agenda, even if your shoe laces are tied together.

This aspect of headship reminds me of the time that Morecambe and Wise had André Previn on their programme. Eric Morecambe played a piece of music on the piano. It was a grotesque mess. André Previn screwed his face up at the cacophony, accusing Morecambe of playing the wrong notes. 'I am playing the right notes', Morecambe insisted indignantly, 'but not necessarily in the right order'.

The world of music also offers rich comparisons with being a head teacher. One role is that of 'head as Viennese conductor'. There is a tradition in Vienna of the conductor, usually a talented violinist, joining in Strauss waltzes, by waving his bow and playing his violin with the orchestra. I am not sure what double bass or tuba playing conductors do in the circumstances, but the evident enjoyment of the leader is infectious.

The enthusiastic participant Viennese conductor role has become harder to play, and many heads lament having less time to teach classes than they once had. A weak substitute is that of the 'singing telegram', whereby the head joins in activities on an occasional basis, when asked, often as part of a celebration or special event.

The story is told of the postman who took a telegram to a house. 'Will you sing it to me?', the recipient asked. 'I'm afraid this is not a singing telegram service, sir', the postman replied. 'Oh go on', the man insisted, 'just this once'. 'Very well', the postman replied reluctantly, 'Di dum di dum di dum. Your Auntie Mary's dead'.

Being the bearer of bad tidings is a difficult chore, especially when the financial situation becomes known and decisions about cutbacks or staff redundancies have to be announced. Many heads are very good communicators, but there is no way that some pieces of bad news can be dressed up to make them good news. 'The bad news is – we've got no money. But the good news is – we won't have to worry about how to spend it'.

All that said, the truth is that giving effective leadership in education has never been more important. A few years ago I knew a man who was a redcoat in a holiday camp. His hardest job was to sing 'Good Morning campers' the day after working into the early hours and then having a few drinks to relax. Next morning, headache and all, smiling throughout, he would trill the banal lyrics through clenched teeth.

The next time you see a head beaming and singing vigorously 'For those in peril' during morning assembly, just remember it might be someone valiantly playing the role of 'head teacher as hung over redcoat'.

1 November 1996

Read all about the lost register drama

Do not be surprised, during the next few months, if every single aspect of education that comes into the news, for whatever reason and however trivial, is seized upon as part of the hysterical pre-election fever that has gripped the nation.

It is the 'Chicken Licken' phenomenon. Any piddling story about education will soon be blasted across the land as further evidence that the sky has fallen in and that the whole country has gone to the dogs. Only the most drastic measures, like a return to thumbscrews and the rack, can possibly save us from moral collapse.

So the message is clear. Try at all costs not to mislay your dinner register. In these neurotic times, it could move from a minor mishap to a national tragedy within hours, for the steps to notoriety are as predictable as they are unstoppable.

Stage 1 is that 'TEACHER LOSES DINNER REGISTER' will immediately be a front-page headline in the *Swineshire Globe*.

'A fresh disaster has hit crisis-torn Swineshire schools. Late yesterday afternoon Mrs Mavis Scattergood (42), Year 2 teacher at Swineshire County Primary School, mislaid her dinner register. 'I don't know what happened exactly', she confessed, 'I gave it to Darren Rowbottom to take to the school office and it just seems to have disappeared'.

Mrs Scattergood was said to be distraught last night and unwilling to comment further on the incident. Friends said she had gone into hiding. Chairman of the school governors, quarry owner Ned Nock (59), assured reporters that no stone would be left unturned.

Swineshire Primary School head teacher Bill Scroggins (48, looks 78) said that as far as he was concerned it was a one-off. 'Mavis Scattergood is a very professional teacher who has never been in any trouble before and I shall be standing by her' he said in her defence'.

Stage 2 is that the story is then picked up by the national press under headlines like 'Another school in chaos', 'The shame of our lost dinner registers', and 'Trendy teacher loses vital papers'.

The Daily Bazooka leads off with 'Pert sexy brunette Mavis Scattergood (42) has lost her kit etc.', while the Weekly Bore puts together a four-page special on how teachers have failed the nation.

'On the surface it may seem like a trivial matter, but the loss of dinner registers is symptomatic of the deep malaise affecting the whole of the teaching profession. No longer can teachers be relied upon to collect and report culinary statistics. This once proud profession, dominated by a post-Plowden progressive ideology, has finally reaped the consequences of its 'anything goes' philosophy. Anything does indeed go, including the dinner register'.

By now the greatest circus of the late millennium is irrevocably on the march. Only the bishops, bless them, remain sane. The rest of the acrobats cartwheel all over the stage.

The Society for Raving Prejudice Against Anything (president Charles Farnes-Barnes, spokesman Charles Farnes-Barnes, sole member Charles Farnes-Barnes) fulminates on every channel. Dead politicians are disinterred and propped up against a radiator in the studio to nod posthumous disapproval of the 20th century.

Meanwhile a group of MPs issues a statement that caning should be reintroduced for teachers who mislay dinner registers and that none of this would have happened if Mrs Scattergood had worn a crinoline and her head teacher had been dressed in spats, a waistcoat and a top hat.

The government, desperate to retain power until May 1st, promises to consider adding clauses on caning teachers who mislay dinner registers to its Education Bill. Press speculation mounts about whether this will be sufficient to appease the Euro-sceptics and whether John Major still has a grip on his party.

Ministers assure us that the loss of any document, let alone one as important as the dinner register, has always been close to its heart, and the late great Kenneth Baker might even be brought out of the cupboard to add a few more clauses to his Dangerous Dogs Act so it covers teachers as well.

Opposition parties claim this is not tough enough and is too little too late. The Lib Dems are prepared to put up taxes to cover proper collection of gastronomic data, but Labour will do it within existing resources. The Referendum Party promises to hold a referendum on the motion 'Should teachers lose their control of dinner registers or should .... (add your own form of words)'.

There are one hour in-depth specials on the whole matter on Newsnight, Panorama, World in Action, and a breath of fresh air in Floyd on Dinner Registers ('Who gives a toss about the bloody dinner register, this is a damn good claret').

Wars, famines, disasters, the machinations of dictators in faraway lands are all displaced from the top of the news agenda as the nation contemplates the greatest issue facing mankind – what happened to Mavis Scattergood's dinner register and how could it have been prevented?

Finally the *Swineshire Globe* discovers that the dinner register has turned up in Darren Rowbottom's schoolbag. He had put it there by mistake and forgotten about it. For a while no-one notices, but slowly the circus pulls down its marquees, packs its chattels and moves camp. No-one is interested any longer in Mavis Scattergood, the head teacher's waistcoat or lack of it, the fate of dinner registers. It is all now passé, post orgasm.

So if you work in education, then for the next six months, until the polling booths close at one minute past ten on May 1st or whenever, don't hiccup, don't cough, don't sneeze, don't trip over your own feet, don't even breathe.

If you need to burp, drive out to the moors, make sure you are not followed, and do it discreetly and in private. Tell no-one. You have been warned.

15 November 1996

Nostalgia for the 'bad old days'

When I was a lad we all behaved ourselves in school. The lessons were full of factual information which we learned assiduously. We respected our teachers and we did three hours of homework every night. Nobody ever messed around in class.

In those days anybody who stepped out of line was given the cane. In fact you got caned even if you did not misbehave, just in case. On Sunday we all went to church to pray for forgiveness, albeit for sins we had never committed, because we were so perfect.

As a result Britain was the most highly educated and successful nation since the dawn of time. We bestrode the world like a Colossus, led by the most immaculate leaders ...

I'm sorry, I can't go on with this. Did loads of homework every night? Never messed around? Highly educated and successful? It is complete and utter tripe. I just fancied having a little bask in that warm wave of nostalgia which engulfs the nation.

Education has been criticised throughout this year. The Secretary of State expressed the concern of many universities over 'deficiencies in the general education and in the grasp of the English language of the candidates coming to them from schools'. One major employer found that the literacy of thousands of newly recruited employees was so poor that they had to lay on special classes and produce their own literacy textbook.

It got worse. The Chief Inspector wrote: 'Teachers are, as a rule, uncultured and imperfectly educated'. A devastating critique of special needs teaching led to a new Act of Parliament being proposed, because so many SEN children were receiving an inadequate education. A senior civil servant wrote a damning report saying that our education system was much poorer than that of our European competitors.

Morality and discipline were also criticised in the press. The Prime Minister described his own school as 'the greatest pagan school in Christendom'. Another school had to call in the army as the children had barricaded themselves in. Then there was that dreadful group of pupils who blew off the head teacher's door with explosives.

Oops! I'm sorry. I seem must have got things mixed up. These are all events that actually happened in the 'good old days'. It was Sir David Eccles in 1960 who reinforced universities' concerns about candidates' use of English. The employer who had to teach thousands of recruits to read and write was the Army in 1943, the even better old days.

The Chief Inspector who called teachers 'imperfectly educated' was Mr Holmes in 1905. The Act of Parliament demanded for special needs was the 1899 Defective and Epileptic Children Act, while the civil servant who envied Europe was Robert Morant in 1898.

Earlier still, in the fantastically good old days, Gladstone was the Prime Minister who described 1820s Eton as 'pagan', and two companies of soldiers with fixed bayonets were brought in to recapture Winchester in 1818. The pupils of Rugby blew off the head teacher's door with gunpowder in 1797. It all makes the odd V sign at the Ridings School look like St Francis of Assisi's birthday party.

So why do we nostalge? Why do we allow ourselves to be tormented about the glories of the past? It is no use blaming the mass media. They are simply recognising a primeval drive to believe that the world is doomed, discipline is hopeless and standards are dropping through the floor.

The first reason is the 'we'll all be murdered in our beds' explanation. Just as children like to frighten themselves with tales of ghosts and bogeymen, so adults create their equivalent sources of imagined terror. We will grow old and be surrounded by witless youth, incapable of earning a living, coping with adversity, or providing for our frailty.

Come a nuclear disaster, it is believed, today's children would be unable to do what we could all do in our youth, like boil three pairs of wellingtons to make a nourishing stew, carve a

Ford Transit van out of a few matchsticks, knit a marquee from old socks. Instead they would wander round after the devastation looking for the Radio Times and complaining that their tea wasn't ready.

We, meanwhile, would starve to death while they chattered about Gazza's latest hair style, mugged the elderly and listened to what was left of their CD collection on their Walkman. It is rubbish, of course. Many of today's young people are full of initiative. They would be just as resourceful as we like to think we were, but then this is not a rational matter.

The second reason is that for over a decade some ministers exaggerated criticisms of education to justify their policies. There is no need to reform education if it is doing well, so repeat over and over the message of failure. Then you can ride up on your white horse, snatch a grateful public from the jaws of advancing voracious doom, and get re-elected.

The fact of the matter is that, in this imagined period of disaster, we have had unparalleled political interference in education. Laws have been passed spelling out the tiniest detail of curriculum, assessment, finance, how to fill in a school report or an attendance register. Some politicians would like to prescribe the size of your elbow patches, the length of your skirt and the colour of your Hush Puppies.

Fortunately people are not entirely fooled. In opinion polls teachers now come higher than they used to in public esteem, up in the Premier League with doctors, whereas politicians are in danger of relegation at the bottom of the Scumbag League.

This is equally unfair on them. The incompetent or malevolent few have created a bad image for the many good and well intended politicians. To paraphrase Mark Twain, 'First God made idiots. This was just for practice. Then he made certain public figures'.

29 November 1996

Uncle Ted's special stocking fillers

BUMPER XMAS SUPPLEMENT

Have you run out of ideas for the festive season? Are you desperately trying to decide what present to buy a teacher suffering from December blues, or what to do after your Christmas dinner? Then this special supplement is packed with ideas just for you.

GIFTS
For him
OFSTED whoopee cushion
Complete with picture of Registered Inspector. Slip it under someone's chair cushion and the words 'generally sound' come out in rasping flatulent tones as he sits down. Mass hilarity. No staffroom is complete without one. £4.99, OFSTED Inflatables Plc.

For her
Inflatable Chief Inspector
Life-size balloon of Chris Woodhead. Blow it up, let go of it, and watch him fizz round and round the room until empty. Hours of harmless therapeutic fun. £14.99. OFSTED Inflatables Plc.

For head teachers
League table mirror
Highly polished mirror with tasteful mahogany surround. Hold it underneath any league table of school examination results, truancy scores or whatever, and hey presto! Suddenly, in the reflection, the bottom schools come top of the league. No action plan needed. Saves months of anguish. £19.99. Tricky Stats & Co.

BOOKS

Gone To The Dogs (Volumes 1 – 10)
Rhodes Boyson's thesaurus of comments on examination results. Handy for when GCSE and A level results come out each August. Contains several thousand well-known phrases and sayings, going back to Chaucer's time and beyond, meaning 'Standards have fallen'. Includes useful variants like 'Standards have fallen, forsooth' (Shakespeare) and 'Ye country has gone to ye dogs' (Henry VIII). £29.99 per volume. Blusterbooks.

Was I Bloody Brilliant, Or Was I Bloody Brilliant?
Kenneth Baker's modest account of how he reformed education, climbed Everest wearing only a jock strap, and scored seventeen goals during extra time to win the World Cup for England in 1966. Now remaindered, so bumper value. 49p. Fantasy Island Publishers.

CD ROMs

The Governors
Any group of school governors of up to 20 can play. All you do is feed in the topics on the agenda, like 'Head teacher's report', or 'Financial forward plan', and the computer generates a totally fictitious record of the business. Why waste valuable time on a meeting? You simply turn up for the tea and biscuits and let the head and chairman make up the minutes, as they would have done anyway! £29.99. Machiavelli Interactive Technology.

Kwality Assurance
Brilliant CD ROM game making the very best of new interactive technology. Superb graphics and musical sound effects. You will never again need to write another mission statement, school policy statement, or action plan. Simply key in a title. The program automatically writes you a document of any desired length in fluent Kwalispeak. Even native speakers of Kwalispeak cannot tell it from the real thing. ('It certainly delivered my baseline kwality objectives in a very downsized, cost-effective and time-constrained manner', Mr I Robot-Automaton, head teacher, Conveyor Belt High School). £99.99. Kwality Games Inc.

CHRISTMAS ON TV
Carry On Nursery Voucher
All the old favourites from the 'Carry On' team are back on screen again. This time nursery school head Sid James, desperate to pass muster on his 'Desirable Learning Outcomes' and qualify for nursery vouchers to pay off his gambling debts, tries to impress a team of three-day trained nursery inspectors, led by Kenneth Williams. Pure farce.

Cast

Reggie Ofsted	Kenneth Williams
Desperate Dan	Sid James
Gillian Shephard	Hattie Jacques
John Major (as a boy and as a man)	The Krankies

POST-CHRISTMAS QUESTIONS
Question I must say that a lot of the flak aimed at politicians is, in my view, unjustified. We have just sent out letters of invitation for our Prize Giving in the New Year, and the first three acceptances came, by return of post, from the Conservative, Labour and Liberal Democrat candidates. It makes you wonder what drives these public-spirited people, if they can find time in a busy schedule to come to our school.

Answer A general election.

Question My grandmother used up turkey leftovers in a nourishing dish called Shephard's Pie. Do you have the recipe?

Answer The key ingredient of Shephard's Pie is the right wing, which determines the content of this dish. Take the right wing. Surround it with vegetables. Allow to simmer but not to boil. Smile all the while, but watch that the top doesn't get too crusty. Serve with marshmallow and fruitcake.

Question My two year old son got a box of marzipan chickens for Christmas. The trouble is, he doesn't like marzipan, so he pulled all the heads off them and now nobody else wants to eat them. What on earth can I do with a load of headless chickens?

Answer Run the country.

13 December 1996

Comic relief as darkness descends

Some years improve with age. Unfortunately 1996 got dafter as the months went by. What would have been regarded as hysterical in January became normal by October, as the time for a general election drew closer. In the end it is a merciful relief that January will count towards 1997, otherwise 1996 could have become embarrassing.

As the dark nights descend I welcome any comic relief, so the clamour for a dress code for teachers offered rich pickings. I combed the schools of the land, eagerly looking for these staffrooms full of far out hippies. It was disappointing to find so many soberly dressed teachers. Saint Michael seemed to be far more popular than Saint Scruff.

The fuss about bringing back the cane was similar. What should have been a legitimate and straightforward debate about moral education suddenly became a trial of strength. The discussion rapidly shifted to the reintroduction of corporal punishment, as some advocates of caning urged John Major to defy the European Parliament.

The reason that caning was abolished in this country is because of the European Convention on Human Rights, which we have accepted. It rules as illegal any punishment that is 'inhuman or degrading'. It is exactly the same clause that bans torture or police brutality. If an adult were permitted, on witnessing misbehaviour, to take a stick and beat a child, then a policeman might equally be allowed to clonk a shoplifter with a truncheon.

The prospects for 1997 do not, therefore, seem all that good. With a general election due, the likelihood of a rational discussion on educational issues in the first half of the year is low. This is a pity, as planning for the 21st century version of the national curriculum will have to start in earnest.

The present curriculum runs until the year 2000. A new one must be communicated to schools in good time, so the revised version will have to be agreed in principle by late 1998. That means starting the consultation process in Spring 1997. It would be dreadful if what should be a cool intelligent look at a sensible and imaginative curriculum for the next millennium were to be clouded by pre-election political and ideological hysteria.

After eight years of experience with the national curriculum, there will be no shortage of informed advice, as opposed to guesswork. I only hope that politicians will listen this time. Maybe the inescapable commotion that will accompany the start of the rethink will soon subside and be replaced by a mixture of pragmatism and imagination.

Some of 1997 is all too predictable. In April at least one person attending a teacher union conference will say, 'I am a teacher, not a social worker'. In mid and late August the annual A level and GCSE results will be published. The overall pass rates will have gone up by one per cent, while the number of A level entries in chemistry and physics will have gone down yet again. The headlines in the national press will say that standards have fallen irrespective of whether there are more or fewer passes.

By November the annual league tables will be published. The national test scores for eleven year olds will have gone up again (but standards will still have fallen, according to critics). There will be freezing fog and heavy snowfalls before Christmas. Trendy teachers, absence of caning, lack of a dress code and progressive methods will be blamed.

The new Parliament will take us into the 21st century. My hopes for education are simple. There are five things I should like to see.

An end to the 'Me Tarzan, you scum' style of national management perfected by Kenneth Baker-Clarke-Patten. It is demeaning to any profession, let alone one like teaching that is supposed to have a bit of imagination and initiative, to be subjected to constant humiliation. It would barely be tolerable if the leader were a genius, but this disastrous macho style was developed by a constellation of unalloyed prats. Even though Gillian Shephard has tried to be different, the general lack of trust of the teaching profession still remains. Only when it ends will the climate improve.

The instant incineration of much of the paperwork and bureaucracy that has sapped precious time and energy away from the classroom. If fed into power stations it would heat several medium-sized cities for weeks. Lack of trust lies beneath this affliction too. If you are suspicious of people, you make them write everything down, so you can keep a check on their activities. Paper becomes a god. Sadly it can also become a substitute for action, rather than the cause of it.

More positive press coverage of education. Not for one moment should there be any restraint, in a free society, on legitimate criticism of poor performance. All I am asking for is a fair-minded account of what is happening in education. In one recent international comparison we came high in science and low in maths. Some accounts only mentioned the maths. Examination coursework has ensured that pupils have to work throughout the two years of their GCSE or A level, not just put in a spurt before the exams, as many of their parents did. Yet coursework gets an almost universally bad press. One or two journalists should also try to write a few columns without using the word 'trendy'. Hard, I know, but worth the effort.

An end to the market-mad philosophy that tries to set school against school, pupil against pupil and teacher against teacher. Competition is sometimes valuable, but in most of daily life co-operation is more important. Sensible teachers and heads have minimised the bad effects of this fabricated strife and conflict, but it has not done much for children with special needs, in danger of being seen as lepers.

Pigs should fly.

Happy New Year.

27 December 1996

Awake, sleeping beauties of jargon

There is a new craze for dealing with stress. It is known as the 'flotation tank'. You pay your fee, and then lie in an enclosed tank of warm salt water and simply float there, in darkness and silence, for a period of time. It is said to be good therapy for you.

Some people, apparently, are so overwhelmed after floating in the tank for a while, they are unable to speak coherently when they emerge. For the last few years I have managed to obtain the same degree of paralytic non-alcoholic intoxication at no cost. I just sit and read Government documents. It switches off time and turns the brain to a fine mulch.

It was amusing, therefore, to read that 130 people involved in the writing of National Vocational Qualifications had been sent on courses to teach them how to write in plain English. The cost was a somewhat less hilarious £116,000.

At about £900 a head I wonder if it included an hour in the flotation tank. I hope the food was good. Or, as the NVQ writers themselves would have put it, before their plain English course, 'I express the desire that the consumables and comestibles presented to the aforementioned clients were completely compliant with the operational specification'.

All this riveting information was given in a written parliamentary answer. A team of researchers had fed all 2 million words found in NVQ documents into a computer, compared them with a vast store of articles from newspapers, broadcasts and books, and come to the conclusion that the language was often opaque and ambiguous. The conclusion was as unexpected as the discovery that an elephant is bigger than a gnat.

The whole saga left me asking more questions than were answered in the report. For example: did it really need as many as 130 people to hand craft all that tortuous bureaucratic rubbish? Could not two or three of them have achieved the same effect with a dictionary and a random number generator?

Moreover, how on earth did 130 people avoid getting in each other's way? Did they work in teams of ten and agree to write each tenth word? ('I'll write 'performance', if you lot then go on to pen 'criteria', 'underpinning', 'scrimbleboobs' and the rest').

In terms of the ethics of the research involved: was it fair to the computer to feed 2 million words of NVQ-speak into it? It is like asking someone to eat 2 million marshmallows to see if they are sweet. Is there no Bill of Rights for computers, no pressure group acting on their behalf? Was the computer off sick for several days afterwards?

Was there any need to do research into the complexity of NVQ terminology in the first place? All you have to do is ask teachers or students who have ever taught or studied the things. Any punter would have offered the same single unambiguous word in reply, which in NVQ-speak would be 'excreta of the male bovine organism'.

It seems bizarre that here we are in Britain, desperately trying to improve the knowledge and skill of thousands of experienced workers and trainees and the biggest obstacle is not the intellectual toughness of the course, but the bureaucratic complexity of the documents.

I wonder what Government documents will look like in future, now that the writers have been purified. I must admit to a tinge of sadness that these mighty wordsmiths, formerly capable of scoring a straight 100 on the most powerful bullshit-ometers in the Universe, will now, like Samson shorn of his locks, whimper away in plain English.

Goodbye to 'action tasks and originate evidence'. Farewell to 'undertake rectifying actions'. Hello to 'do things' and 'correct mistakes'.

The requirements for the new NVQ level 5 in 'Transplant Surgery' will now read:

Step 1   Carve open chest.
Step 2   Snip out old heart.
Step 3   Slot in new heart.
Step 4   Stitch everything up.
Step 5   Collect surgeon's badge.

However, all is not lost. When people's skills are no longer needed they usually face two choices. The first is to retrain, which is what the NVQ-smiths have had to do. The second, and sometimes better option, is to find another job where you can still use your old skills. I have the very solution, a happy marriage between one problem, and another.

In view of the complaints that some primary school reading materials are not demanding enough, why not let redundant or unretrainable NVQ employees spend an hour or two in the flotation tank and then re-write some of the great fairy stories and nursery rhymes in NVQ-speak? They could toughen them up a bit.

In future young children throughout the land could skip around primary school playgrounds and classrooms singing NVQ songs and rhymes. Stressed parents and teachers would no longer need a flotation tank, as they listened happily to their children trilling the new version of Baa Baa Black Sheep, which would read as follows:

'O repeated wavering bleat of the ruminant mammal of the genus 'Ovis',
Are you in possession of any quantity of light-textured hirsute epidermis?'
'Double affirmative, respected titular prefix. A triad of plethoric flexible receptacles containing the requisite material.
A singularity for the predominant masculine personage,
A singularity for the predominant feminine personage,
And a singularity for the homunculus who resides at the nether extremity of the narrow highway'.

Ah, they don't write them like that any more.

10 January 1997

Get out before they rewrite the plot

Do you remember those prisoner-of-war camp films, like The Great Escape, The Wooden Horse and Colditz? They were created to satisfy huge post-war nostalgia for heroes, as peace time began to seem boring. Many clean cut matinee idols, along with a few working class scruff stereotypes, made their first successful screen appearance in them.

The upper crust lantern jawed types played the officers, most of whom escaped through some clever ruse. The uncouth proles did all the digging and then got mowed down by the guards, while the toffs made their getaway to the posh Swiss skiing resort where some of their chums were waiting with gin and tonics and a replacement Saville Row wardrobe.

I was reminded of this Pinewood and Hollywood genre by the language used to describe the Government's plans to fore-close on the teachers' early retirement scheme. It was rich in the metaphors of prisoner-of-war camp escapes, as teachers 'made a bolt for freedom' before the 'escape routes are sealed off' in March.

Retirement, early or otherwise, is a very important issue for all professions. It has always seemed to me to be a stupid arrangement that people are expected to work flat out until the day they are 65 and then do absolutely nothing from the following day onwards. It is not a very intelligent way to plan a life.

Much better would be to have a programme of phased retire-ment for those who want it. It ought to be possible to devise a flexible scheme for teachers and others aged between 50 and 65, or even 70. Someone could, in the first stage, teach three quarters of the time and take a one quarter pension, then move to a fifty-fifty work and pension split, and, in the final phase, perhaps even to three quarters pension and one quarter work.

Thousands of people in many fields now practise what is sometimes called 'portfolio' working, that is putting together more than one type of activity. I should hate to see an army of itinerant semi-retired teachers all in the same school, but I cannot believe that the option of phased retirement for some teachers who would prefer it is inconceivable.

Indeed, it would be a good way of keeping alive some of the expertise that is currently being lost. Teachers who move on to part-time teaching in the later stages of their career often find it refreshing, and pupils get the benefit of their less stressed approach.

With an impending teacher shortage of huge proportions, schools might welcome the flexibility of being able to hire someone for a chunk of the week, especially in shortage areas. The danger that some early retired teachers might lose interest is no greater than the possibility of unretired teachers burning out through stress. Safeguards could be put in place to see off those who did not fulfil their part-time contract properly.

It is sad that a profession that normally thrives on the dedication and enthusiasm of its members has been brought to a position where so many now want to quit. When I first started teaching one member of staff decided to pack in at the age of 61. 'What's up with him?', people whispered, 'Has he flipped? Is he ill?'. Today, when someone carries on to 65, as only a quarter of teachers actually do, the whisperers ask: 'What's up with her? Has she flipped? Hasn't she spotted that most of her contemporaries left years ago?'.

Maybe the next generation of films will be all about teachers breaking out. I have already begun work on the film script of my new novel, just in case.

Escape from Stalag Luft XIII Comprehensive School (and Community College)

'Right chaps', said Spiffy (Deputy head, pastoral care and rooms timetable), 'It's time to go over the top'. The motley assortment of Escape Committee members slowly sipped down their plastic cups of weak coffee and came to order.

'Do we have to meet in the boiler room, Spiffy?', grunted 'Kipper' Tye (P.E and remedial metalwork).

'Keep your voice down you fool', Spiffy hissed. 'The goons from the Teacher Escape Police will hear you'. Heavy footsteps echoed down the corridor outside. Hearts stopped as they held their breath.

'Crikey, that was a close one'. There was an audible sigh of relief as the footsteps died away. 'Let's go through the escape plans one by one', said Spiffy.

'Well the wooden horse idea didn't work', Taffy Welshman (geography and league tables) groaned. 'We got three of the staff inside the vaulting horse. Year 9 had dug the tunnel as part of their geography project, see, only they fell down on their national curriculum geography skills 3d, 'use and interpret maps and plans at a variety of scales'. Instead of ten metres to the perimeter fence, they dug it ten kilometres to the Swinesville sewage farm. Nasty ending that was'.

Suddenly the door to the boiler room burst open. A long sinister shadow fell across the bare floor. 'Vot hev ve here?'. The chilling sarcastic tones of Teacher Escape Police Officer Gerry Gauleiter struck terror into their marrow. Empty plastic cups, all marked 'Swinesville LEA Privatised Catering Services Plc', clattered from limp hands.

'So Tommy. You sink you can escape, heh?', he barked.

'Cripes, what do we do now, Spiffy?', Taffy asked as panic paralysed his limbs.

Spiffy took control. Not for nothing had he been schooled at Oxbridge (Secondary Modern). 'Well, I suggest we boycott Key Stage 3 tests, refuse to supervise student teachers, and if that fails, we seek a judicial review'.

Gerry German blinked. Then he recovered his composure. 'If you vish to leave, zen you or ze school must pay for it', he hissed. 'Ve hev vays of making you teach'......

24 January 1997

The very model of a sergeant-major general

Boing, boing, boing. Look out! There goes the elastic school, bouncing on its eccentric path across the landscape. Just when everyone thought that the Loonytunes section of Government policy making had been quietly parked in the nearest deep freeze, out comes a whole raft of new crazy horse right-wing wheezes.

The right-wing of Government policy making has begun to flap so vigorously, it is small wonder that the whole beast is going round in circles. Meanwhile its eyeballs rotate eerily in the same direction, like some huge ungainly Alice in Wonderland nursery mobile.

Over the next few weeks stand by for a torrent of demented proposals from the dogmatic free market ideologues in the Government, from elastic schools to privatised canes inlaid with little music boxes that play 'Land of Hope and Glory' when used.

The belief that schools can expand and contract at the flick of a switch has been and gone a few times during the last few years. It is based on the right-wing utopian idea that a 'free market' in education would solve all problems of choice and quality. According to this nutty philosophy, any school that is popular would simply expand indefinitely at the expense of its neighbours, thereby putting them out of business if they failed to compete.

The elastic school idea is all very well provided there is stability and schools remain roughly equal in public esteem. Any significant changes, however, and chaos would ensue. A new head teacher, a new fad or fashion, and the result is dystopia, the exact opposite of utopian paradise.

What is forgotten in this mad quest for a return to 19th century *laissez-faire* liberalism, is that the commercial market can sometimes produce unintended and disastrous consequences. For example, in the commercial world businesses tend to get bigger, as smaller firms go bust and the giants then slug it out. Do we want bigger schools? More to the point, do we want school bankruptcies on a wide scale?

Let us assume that the town of Dystopia has six high schools, each containing about 1,000 pupils. Parents are allowed to send their children to any of the six and the school must expand to accommodate them.

After a while two schools become very popular, two remain medium sized, and two less popular schools shut down, as their numbers fall. Parents now only have a choice of four schools instead of six. Eventually two giant schools with 3,000 pupils replace the four, but then become unpopular because of their large scale. Parents ask for more schools to be built of a manageable size.

Will we really be willing to fund lots of new schools, face up to empty and unused buildings on a large scale? Imagine the spectacle of endless Portakabins, redundant in one area but needed in another, cruising up and down motorways, pursued by thousands of teachers driving around looking for jobs in elastic schools. What if the market produced a single Dystopia High School with 6,000 pupils?

The marketeers' answer to this, of course, is either that it would never happen, or that, if it did come about, this must be what parents wanted. In theory the free market sorts out all the problems. The same argument used to be put forward about unregulated field centres. The bad would close down, it was said, as schools discovered they were no good. Sadly, it took the Lyme Bay canoe tragedy to explode the myth that the market can control quality.

Another right-wing chuckler is the proposal to invest large sums of money in school cadet corps. Even though neither John Major nor Michael Portillo chose to join their own school military units, they seem to believe that huge sums of public cash should be injected to make this the most favoured voluntary school activity, outrageous when you think of the many worthwhile school activities that are starved of funding.

It seems bizarre, after the Dunblane tragedy, that it is warfare preparation which is identified as the top priority for financial support. In the debates about the 1944 Education Bill a Mr Wakefield MP asked if pupils should be required to practise shooting on a miniature rifle range. R A Butler, the sensible minister of the time, wisely rejected the idea, even in time of war, saying that politicians should not interfere in schools.

It is all symptomatic of the quest for an imagined bygone age of great and magnificent glory, when well scrubbed children sat obediently in rows, eagerly learning their tables up to a thousand times a thousand, and no-one ever wrote the word 'accommodation' with a missing letter 'c' or 'm'.

However, I don't want to be a spoilsport. I sometimes feel guilty arguing against a return to the 19th century if that is what people really want. Perhaps typhoid, squalor, hypocrisy and rickets were a lot more fun than we realise. Let us go the whole hog with Major and Portillo on the militia idea. Since it is a right-wing idea, pupils could do their marching drill up and down the school playground to the command of 'Right – right – right'.

Children could start in nursery schools in a regiment of the Portillinos, striving to meet their 'desirable learning outcomes' in khaki uniforms. Once in primary school they could join a legion of the Portillettes. Secondary school militia members would belong to a crack squad of Portillons. 'Look out! Here come the Portillons'. It has an impressive ring to it, like the terrifying Klingons in Star Trek.

Best of all, the army of khaki-clad Portillinos, Portillettes and Portillons would provide a lasting memorial to John Major's contribution to education. The Prime Minister could become their leader and role model and, like Lord Baden-Powell, founder of the scout and guide movement, be remembered to the end of time – as Major Major.

7 February 1997

Fairy tales for the Loonytune league

There is a view of life, put forward by the Government and endorsed by some of its agencies, that teachers, and indeed children, are best motivated by the 'blame and shame' approach to education. Hence the constant stress on the discipline of the market and the benefits of competition. The philosophy goes back to mediaeval times: make them run the obstacle course and if they fall down, put them in the stocks.

In the full list of madcap right-wing free market ideas launched on the world between now and the general election, John Major's proposal to publish school league tables for seven year olds can be entered officially as Loonytunes number 18a. It may actually be 20b, or even 22c, I am rapidly losing count.

Life is a mixture of competition and collaboration, but the view that teachers are only driven by competition is pure folly. The belief that thousands of professional people are positively slavering with pleasure at the prospect of thumping hell out of the opposition in primary school league tables, and that this alone will spur them on to improve, is the credo of the halfwit, if that is not too generous an estimate of Major's brain power.

Even worse is the assumption that children themselves will work harder and learn more because of league tables. I cannot see many six and seven year olds showing much interest in promotion and relegation struggles, or, when sponsorship begins to play its part, giving a fig who wins the Chocky Drop League championship trophy.

All that the blame and shame culture has produced so far is a casualty list of stressed teachers who seek to quit the profession. The definitive history of education in 20th century Britain will one day denounce this market mad period, just as history eventually condemned 'payment by results' in the 19th century. League tables, the shaming and humiliation of

37

teachers, as well as the castigation of children who do not achieve highly enough, will be seen as a brief *fin de siècle* aberration.

Those right-wingers who see primary schools as too flaccid and soft argue that league tables will stiffen the culture. I doubt whether the creation of more anxiety among teachers and young children will do anything of the kind.

There is a well known relationship between anxiety and performance. The graph of it is shaped like an inverted letter U. Too little and too much anxiety produce poor performance. If we were not at all anxious when crossing the road, we would fail to look around and be run over. Too much anxiety and we would be scared to leave home.

So will league tables for seven year olds toughen them up? Will the white heat of competition turn Little Twinky into a red clawed tiger? Will parents be delighted to watch their anxious children and their nail-biting teachers frantically trying to cram themselves a notch or two up the league? I doubt it.

I have a better plan to make seven year olds more competitive. I shall re-write all those traditional namby pamby fairy tales that give children a false picture of the dog-eat-dog adult world that the marketeers would like them to inhabit, and prepare them for the many cruel predators and competitors they will eventually meet.

First under the axe will be that old favourite 'The Elves and the Shoemaker' A witless shoemaker tries to sell shoes for the price he paid for the leather. Small wonder that he fell on hard times and had to be rescued by an army of underpaid midgets. In my rewritten version the poor sap will simply go bust and have to sign up as a lay inspector with OFSTED to pay off his debts.

'Jack and the Beanstalk' I like. Good sound capitalist message here. Any giant who nods off with an uninsured golden egg-laying goose on his premises, deserves to have some opportunist pinch it. It's a tough world.

'Little Red Riding Hood' on the other hand will get her come-uppance. Why was she visiting her granny anyway, when she could have been out earning extra cash on a paper round?

If granny is past it, she should have taken out private insurance and been put in a home. In my version the wolf eats both of them and then gets put in charge of a quango or public utility as a reward for his enterprise.

'Cinderella' I quite like. After all, she shows admirable ambition and upward mobility, coming from a humble home and gulling a prince into marrying her, thereby stepping over all the other rats in the rat race. Furthermore she gets extra marks for being prepared to trounce her own sisters when competing for favours. In my version, however, the midnight hour is of no consequence. She simply hires a coach and horses and then defaults on the payments, knowing the firm will probably write them off as a business loss.

Many of the other stories are extremely unsound. The three bears don't bother to charge Goldilocks any rent, and Mummy Bear obviously can't cook a decent plate of porridge, so that particular guest house must go to the wall. Pinocchio's nose should only grow longer if he actually gets caught out when he tells lies. If he gets away with it he should become a cabinet minister.

The most worrying story of all, however, is 'Peter Pan'. Captain Hook is fine, as he can serve as a reminder to all the seven year olds what the National Health Service will offer them if they fail to take out private health insurance when they grow up.

It is Peter Pan himself who is the problem. The poor lad never grows up. If there is one thing that the nation's seven year olds will need to do in this market mad world, it is leave childhood behind – fast.

21 February 1997

Feathers ruffled by birdbrains

I have been invited to a conference being held today in London, but I shall not be going. It is not just the usual high fee (plus VAT) that puts me off. It is the advertising blurb. The conference is called 'The High Reliability School', which sounded interesting enough until I read the details.

'The High Reliability Schools Project is an attempt to move beyond the goal of relatively successful schools' the invitation trills, 'towards the creation of schools which are absolutely successful and which have eradicated failure'. I'll have a basinful of failure eradication, squire, pray tell me more. It gets even better.

'Using the latest information from the study of highly reliable organisations such as air traffic controllers and nuclear power plants and from school effectiveness and school improvement programmes, an innovatory programme has been designed that aims to ensure high quality educational outcomes for all, in schools which set ambitious targets and which relentlessly push for success'.

Now just a minute, sunshine. I know that the 'relentless push for success' is in vogue, but nuclear power plants, for goodness' sake? We at Chernobyl High School are a touch dubious about that particular model, as are our colleagues at Three Mile Island County Primary School down the road.

Every time our relentless push for success is about to reach its climax, BANG, fifty megatons of irradiated fallout land on your dinner register. 'It's very worrying. It's very worrying', as our two headed caretaker is fond of saying.

Even more worrying was *Newsletter 17*, sent out by the Office for Standards in Education to all its 'contractors' as school inspection teams are affectionately known. I enjoy reading these newsletters, as they are a great curiosity of the English language. On the surface the language is that of jolly insider banter, with little 'nudge nudge' asides, the sort you might get in a school magazine. There the similarity ends, for the rest of it is in written in incomprehensible market-speak.

Newsletter 17 begins with a message from Ofsted's 'Head of Contracts', Mr Silicon Chip, written in characteristic style: 'Perhaps one of the most significant items of news is that the AI initiative is to come to an end in August 1997. There has been a significant growth in the market, helped by the migration of AIs into the market place ...'

What the hell is Mr Chip on about? What are these birds that have migrated into the market square? Are we talking about inspectors here, or budgerigars?

For those not fluent in Ofstedspeak, the term 'AI' does not mean 'artificial insemination'. It stands for 'Additional Inspector', i.e. head teachers who were pulled out of their school for a year to supplement school inspection teams. Now many of them have been found to be surplus to requirements, so they have simply been sent back to their school half way through the year. Perhaps it was all part of Ofsted's 'relentless push for success', presumably based on the nuclear fission model – if it overheats, blow it up.

'Hello. It's little me again', the heads had to say to the school's acting head and staff as they reappeared in their schools several months before expected. Some of the more embarrassed obviously decided to migrate. Presumably they hung a sign on their door, saying not 'Gone fishing', but rather 'Migrated to the market place. Signed, Tweetie Pie'.

It calls for a rewrite of the celebrated rhyme.

Oh the Grand Old Ofsted boss,
He signed ten thousand men.
He marched them up to the top of the hill
And he marched them down again.
And when they were up, they were up.
So Ofsted at last did the sums.
And when they were only half way through
They were kicked out on their bums.

Getting rid of the Additional Inspectors, or indeed, training them and then finding they migrate to the market place, may turn out to be another nuclear disaster. It confirms that school inspection should become a public service once more instead of a money making business. Local authorities are coming under greater financial pressures, so there is an increasing reluctance to take part in inspections as money gets tighter.

This is for several reasons. First of all a market is a market. It costs the LEA about £400 or so a day for each inspector it employs. To be successful, inspection contractors have to bid nearer £200 per day. It does not take a financial genius to work out the consequences of losing £200 per inspector per day, especially when many are now inspecting outside their own LEA. It is a 'Hello Official Receiver' strategy.

Furthermore schools are increasingly critical of not seeing much of their own local inspectors nowadays, hardly surprising when many are busy Ofstedding around the land. Schools feeling under pressure need all the local help and support they can get.

Meanwhile, back in *Newsletter 17* Mr Chip is blowing a gasket. He is not at all pleased to discover that some naughty inspection teams have won contracts and then had to advertise for team members in the press or get them through what one Ofsted official called 'dating agencies'. I know inspection seems to be all about finding a bird nowadays, but this is ridiculous. 'In plain language, I will not look kindly upon those who make commitments without adequate planning. To do otherwise would be to bring into question their quality assurance procedures', Mr Chip writes angrily.

Who's been a naughty boy then? Pretty Polly?

7 March 1997

Is there an inspector in the house

When I was a child I used to dream of being a member of an illustrious profession. One day I would be walking past the scene of an accident. 'Let me through, I'm a doctor', I would cry and the crowd would melt obediently aside, watching in admiration as I opened my bag of medical equipment, wrought a quick miracle or two, and saved some poor beggar's life.

Back in the real world I became a teacher. Would anyone ever call out in desperation, 'Is there a teacher in the house?', I wondered, eagerly beckoning me through the throng, so I could stroll forward imperiously, clutching my bag of spelling tests and old A level papers, while admiring parents watched me rescue their child from a lifetime of drudgery? Alas, the opportunity never arose.

Nor would it have arisen had I become a head teacher. Would some desperate soul ever have called out 'Is there a head teacher in the house?', at which point I could have rushed forward, picked up all the litter and admonished everybody for untidiness? I fear not.

Once I became an academic the opportunity for instant glamour became even less likely. 'Let me through, I'm a professor of education', I could say proudly. As the crowds melted to one side I would open a bag full of lecture notes, committee minutes and articles on the social correlates of educational performance. I have never had the nerve for it.

Still it could have been worse if I had taken other jobs. 'Is there a chief inspector in the house?', someone might have called out from the crowd, and I would have had to leap up and talk bollocks for half an hour.

Teaching is for stayers, not for sprinters. The fruits of it are planted and harvested day after day, week upon week, not snatched in some spectacular one-off event. Even brilliant

43

teachers who are highly inspirational need a decent period of time to influence their pupils. That is why judging the quality of teaching should be a lot less ham-fisted than it is.

The publication of national primary school league tables provoked a predictable response. As Little Piddlington County Primary School emerged several places higher than Swinesville Junior School, some critics automatically commended the teachers at the former and condemned those at the latter, without bothering to look at the circumstances in which the results had been attained.

'Is there an idiot in the house?', a journalist calls out. 'Let me through, I'm a cretin' cries Henry Halfwit, pushing through the crowd, opening his leather bag of clichés to say that parents should demand that the teachers of Swinesville Juniors pull up their socks, be put on fatigues, or get their cards.

Whatever else league tables do, they tell us little about the quality of teaching in each school. The teachers of Swinesville Juniors may be performing miracles against the odds, while those at Little Piddlington may be cruising along, doing only moderately well with very able and highly motivated pupils. League tables alone will not reveal that hidden story, and no-one with any sense pretends that they do.

There is a high correlation between league table positions and the social class of pupils in each school. Indeed, I am currently working with two university geographers to analyse the most effective use of various social factors when interpreting school test scores.

Although I am in favour of parents knowing the results of school testing programmes, I would still not publish any kind of league tables, even if they have been adjusted to take into account the effects of social background. They are still not the best means of judging the quality of teachers in a school.

Given the complexity of teaching, the many different contexts in which it takes place and the various background factors that influence its outcome, the only feasible way of making an intelligent appraisal of teaching is to assemble what is sometimes called a 'consensus of those able to judge'. So is there an inspector in the house?

Sadly the current inspection model adopted by the Office for Standards in Education is not the answer either, as it is far too mechanical. After the very short training required it is hardly surprising. A week in a hotel (for a £900 fee nowadays) and you get your badge. For what else can you become fully qualified in five days? What on earth can be learned in a week at the Heckmondwike Savoy, other than how to spell 'generally sound'?

Another day or two and you can add further strings to your bow. In a fortnight or so a person can qualify as an inspector of nursery, primary, secondary and special education. 'Let me through, I'm a robot. Let me through, I'm a robot. Let me through, I'm a robot'. Try and get a decent first aid qualification, a pilot's licence, a mountain leadership certificate, or pass your driving test, in just a few days.

When I was in the cubs I had to collect stamps for six months to get my collector's badge. Six bloody months of assiduous cataloguing, mounting, researching, all for one cub badge. If only Ofsted had been around in my childhood I could have spent the same time becoming licensed to inspect teaching, motorway flyovers, hospitals, lorries, fire escapes, jet engines, prisons and intergalactic space craft.

When we set up an intelligent system of inspection which combines national and local strengths, involves both internal and external assessment, on fair and sensible lines, we might be in a better position to judge and improve the quality of teaching. While it is treated as a single low level skill, capable of being league tabled, there is little hope.

Is there an inspiration in the house?

21 March 1997

Head feels curse of the Scottish play

The other evening I went to watch a school play. It celebrated the long history of the school, stretching back to the early origins of education in the town in the 16th century. It was great fun and performers and audience enjoyed it.

Part way through, the four girls on stage lost track of their words. Professional actors would no doubt have employed some skilful fudge, and many adult performers would have been in a state of deep panic, but these four simply walked off the stage, held an animated conversation in the wings, and then returned as if nothing had happened. It was done with great aplomb and nobody minded in the least.

The four girls will recall that event in the middle of the next century, when they are in their sixties. Of all the things that happen in a busy school life, it is often the unexpected and hilarious cock-ups at concerts, plays and performances of one kind or another that stay with us. Most adults who ever took part in any public stage show as a child have similar vivid recollections.

I remember as if it was yesterday the unexpected ending of our schoolday version of Macbeth. The high point of the play comes in the very last few moments when Macduff enters carrying Macbeth's head in his hand. Unfortunately the art teacher had spent all term lovingly crafting this grotesque severed head and we had never had it for any of the rehearsals. It only became available for the first public performance.

Macduff strode on to the stage, clutching the fearsome looking gory head, skilfully constructed of wire and papier mache. Parents and actors alike froze, mesmerised, as he moved dramatically to the centre of the apron stage holding it at arm's length.

We on the stage knew that, for the first time, he would be able to cast it contemptuously on to the ground and speak some of Shakespeare's most dramatic lines. He took a deep breath and put on the nearest a schoolboy will ever get to a ferocious look. 'Behold, where stands th'usurper's cursed head', he thundered, before hurling the elaborate prop to the floor.

Bonk, bonk, bonk. The wretched object bounced mightily across the stage, down the steps and then rolled eccentrically past the audience. 'Er, several rows into where the parents are sitting, methinks'. Years afterwards I would meet fellow pupils who would ask if I remembered how audience and cast were convulsed at this memorable event.

A curriculum for the 21st century needs to be wider than the subjects on the timetable, important though these may be. Extra-curricular activities can make as much impact on children as what happens in scheduled class time. Many of us are grateful to our teachers for skills and knowledge we acquired informally. Photography, music, sport, drama, are just some of my own adult interests that were introduced by teachers.

It is partly the relaxed atmosphere that helps make the impact. Conditions for learning are often at their best – volunteers instead of conscripts, high levels of interest and enthusiasm, purposeful rather than, as some children would see it, pointless activities. One teacher I knew used to run a very successful fishing club after school. It was only when he started to teach pupils how to cast a fly during his French lessons that parents got upset.

In most countries there is no tradition of extra-curricular activities. Sadly they also fell into decline in Britain during the 1980s. Many teachers, having given their time freely for years, resented the way they were being treated by the government, so they withdrew from them. Goodwill is like the helium in a balloon. It is usually invisible. Only when it is removed can you see what it actually did.

Fortunately there is now a revival. The charity Education Extra (17 Old Ford Road, London E2 9PL), another brilliant idea from Michael Young, the founder of the Consumer Association, has raised thousands of pounds to help fund out-of-school ventures. School inspections increasingly include references to extra-curricular activities in their reports. It is an important step towards a broad, rather than a drearily narrow view of education.

Some schools have still managed to revive this broader vision of learning in the most unlikely circumstances. One old lag, who boasted proudly that the only extra-curricular activity he was prepared to supervise was a 'wash sir's car after school' society, cheerfully organised a chess club after skilful persuasion by the head. In areas of high crime and danger to pupils, there are examples of children being escorted home in groups by adult volunteers, so that their parents need not worry about safety.

Returning to drama as an extra-curricular activity, it always strikes me as bizarre that we expect children at key stage 3 to have a mature understanding of a Shakespeare play, yet relatively few ever have the opportunity to enact it in any serious and sustained form. It was only when I turned up for the rehearsals, lunch times and after school, that I really appreciated what Shakespeare was on about in Macbeth.

The difference between living the play out of lesson time and doing the classroom version of it was immense. If I had had only the latter I would have hated it. It is the same with other extra-curricular activities. Music out of hours was always more fun than classroom music. Seeing teachers as informal, often funny human beings, made more impact on me than the ritualised versions of them.

So what part did I play in Macbeth? The second witch. It was the eeriest experience of my young life, prancing around muttering threats and trying to frighten people. Only when I later met various education ministers did I realise where Shakespeare must have found the inspiration for his more sinister characters.

4 April 1997

How to kill imagination in one fell swoop

What began in the early 1860s and ended in 1904? What was condemned as a disaster by one of our greatest poets? What do some extremists want to restore in all its glory, despite this?

The answer is the much reviled 19th century system of 'payment by results'. The right wing of the Conservative party wants to bring it back again, as it fits in neatly with the free market notion of survival of the fittest and the weakest going to the wall.

By 1871 schools were being paid an initial government grant of ten shillings per pupil, of which six shillings was for 'average attendance' and four shillings was for passing basic 'grade tests'. There were also payments for younger children and particular subjects, but it was the four shilling bounty for passing tests that killed imagination for over a generation. 'Payment by results' was heavily criticised and eventually ditched.

Ever since that time it has caused great mirth whenever it was mentioned. 'You mean, young children sat chanting slogans that many simply did not understand (slaps thigh with laughter)? And inspectors had to go into classrooms to see whether these children could recite mechanical answers to set questions (collapses on to floor with mirth)? All so that the school could collect another four bob apiece (pounds floor helplessly)?'

The most famous critic of payment by results was Victorian philosopher and poet Matthew Arnold, whose lesser known day job was that of school inspector for 35 years, from 1851 to 1886. In his book 'State Educator', Eric Midwinter gives a moving account of how Arnold hated his job.

Young children were dragged into their classroom, even when they were sick, so the inspector could test them, otherwise the school would lose money, and thus some of its teachers. Arnold compared Victorian schools to the army, saying repeatedly that his role was merely to 'inspect the cartouch-boxes', or cartridge cases.

Now the right wing (Loonytunes policy 149c) wants to restore payment by results. It is yet another example of its comical nostalgia for the 19th century. The 21st century version of this failed system would involve teachers being assessed, and indeed paid, according to their pupils' test results.

This is great news if you work in a highly selective school, rotten news if you teach pupils with learning or behaviour problems. I can just picture the scene.

'Ah, come in Brian. Now we've been taking a close look at your test scores'.

'Oh really, Mr Hardcastle? Good news, I hope'.

'I'm afraid not, Brian. You see, we at Conveyor Belt High School are determined to have the best payment by results system in the country and there are a few problems with your salary assessment'.

'But I got a good report from Ofsted. In fact, the inspector said I was the best 'generally sound' special needs teacher they had ever seen'.

'Indeed. But take the answers to national payment by results test question 3: 'Describe the climate of the polar regions'. The correct answer, according to the national payment by results test handbook, should be: 'The polar caps have tundra and glacial climates, with little precipitation', but I'm afraid Elspeth Scattergood has let you down badly'.

'I don't understand, Mr Hardcastle. I've had the children chanting the answers to all the questions ever since last September'.

'I'm sure you have Brian, but Elspeth writes: 'The police caps have thunder and glazed climbers, with little participation'. That one lost you fifty quid for starters'.

'But she's only got an IQ of 60, and she has got the commas and full stops in the right places, just like we practised'.

'Well it's cost you five big ones on the salary front. Then take Harry Ramsbottom. He puts 'The polar regions ended with the defeat of King Richard the Third by the future Henry the Seventh at Bosworth Fields in 1485'. I mean, it just won't do'.

'But that's only a simple slip, Mr Hardcastle. He's written down the answer to national payment by results test question 4, instead of question 3, by mistake. You know, the one that says 'Describe the ending of the Wars of the Roses'. We've chanted the answers so many times it's not surprising if some of the slower ones get them a bit mixed up'.

'You know the rules, Brian. A genuine pupil mistake loses you fifty quid, but the tariff for answering the wrong question is minus seventy-five'.

'So how does this affect my salary? I don't understand the new pay system'.

'It's simple. Mrs Sanderson, who takes the A stream, will gross forty thousand. Mr Bindweed, who takes the B stream, gets twenty thousand. You and the other special needs staff owe us two hundred quid apiece'.

'But that's not fair, Mr Hardcastle. We've run our socks off all year with some of the most difficult kids in the school'

'I know, Brian. That's why I've got a two stage plan to boost your salary'.

'Two stages? I don't follow'.

'Don't you see? The way to earn more money is to become a better teacher. I'm going to help you become a better teacher, and get a higher salary, in two stages. The first stage is to stop you being a bad teacher, so I'm going to exclude all your special needs kids'.

'What about the second stage?'

'The next step is my master plan to turn you into a good teacher. Mr Major wants to have a grammar school in every town, so we shall become Conveyor Belt Grammar School and you will then automatically become a good teacher'.

'But how will that help the education of my special needs children?'

'Education, Brian? What's education got to do with it? It's results we're talking about'.

18 April 1997

Jockstraps, Star Wars and vodka

Fancy a bit of research? The Teacher Training Agency is offering £2,000 grants for teachers to do research which is 'relevant to improving the quality of teaching and learning in the classroom'. I managed to get a sneak preview of some of the applications.

Project 1 *A study of educational bureaucracy and its artefacts*
This analytical study will involve a rigorous measurement of several of the elements of our school's administrative output. There are three hypotheses:

Hypothesis 1: There will be a positive correlation between the number of A4 sheets in everyone's pigeon hole and the recency of any management course the head has been on.

Hypothesis 2: The combined weight of the school's mission and policy statements exceeds the combined weight of all the school's textbooks.

Hypothesis 3: The accuracy of the minutes of staff meetings is inversely proportional to the IQ of the poor sod who has been fingered to write them.

Budget
Accurate weighing scale   £500
Incinerator   £1,500
Elspeth Scattergood, Upper Swinesville Primary School.

Project 6 *Stress in the science department – an action research project*
Working from an operational hypothesis which states that stress is only amenable to treatment if the right sort of liquid chemical solution can be applied, the science department will be conducting their own action research programme. Stage 1 is to measure accurately several possible indicators of stress, such as heart and blood pressure rates, electrogalvanic skin response, rate of breathing, etc. Stage 2 involves scientific experiments with various liquid chemical solutions in measured doses.

Budget

Measuring instruments   £500
Litre bottles of vodka   £600
Crates of lager   £900

Barry Heineken, Head of Science, Topers' Comprehensive.

Project 14 *The use of incentive schemes in the teaching of reading*

We give a high priority to the teaching of reading in our school. Unfortunately many of the boys in particular seem reluctant to make a start. We propose to investigate the use of a range of incentive schemes to try to improve the reading performance of pupils who make a poor attempt at it. There will be four experimental groups, each offered a different kind of incentive, to see which regime leads to the highest increase in test scores.

Budget

Mars bars   £500
Star Wars figurines £500
Thumbscrews   £500
Rack   £500

Doris Torquemada, Language Co-ordinator, Crushem Infants' School.

Project 21 *The evaluation of school inspections*

A cluster of six primary schools and one secondary school in North Swineshire will be studied over a two year period. Each school will be monitored carefully during its inspection by the Office of Standards in Education. A multi-item questionnaire will be administered before and after the inspection team has been. Key questions will include: 'What is your name?', 'Can you still remember your name?', and 'Have you now decided to change your name?'. Questionnaire responses will be analysed using the most sophisticated techniques available.

Budget

Preparation and analysis of questionnaires   £1,000
'I survived Ofsted' t shirts   £500
Deluxe bullshitometer   £500

Chris Dickhead, Torpid Junior School, North Swineshire.

Project 37 *Personal hygiene and the teaching of physical education*

Several teachers have complained about, how can I put this, the 'aroma' in the vicinity of the male PE staff changing room. The other day one colleague actually fainted as she walked past the gym. A rigorous action research programme will be undertaken in an attempt to rectify this problem by investigating the efficacy of two different possible solutions, one for the PE teachers, the other for the rest of the staff.

Budget

New jock straps   £1,000
Nose clips   £1,000
Albert Reeks, Deputy Head, Olfactory High School.

Project 64 *Understanding educational jargon*

One of our biggest problems is understanding some of the official documents we receive in school. They seem to be so full of jargon that teachers cannot always grasp the main ideas in them. This research project involves the rewriting of all documents that come into the school, to see if staff and governors benefit from having them in plain English. A part-time translator will be employed for several hours each week.

Budget

Fees to translator   £1,500
Anadins for staff and governors   £450
English-Bakerspeak dictionary   £50
Neil Desperandum, Head Teacher, Gibberish Primary School.

Project 129 *Investigating the most effective solution to incompetent teaching*

This is a very successful comprehensive school, but unfortunately there are a few teachers who have become time servers and are not doing their job properly. We propose to investigate and experiment with a number of different ways of first identifying, and then dealing with teachers who are professionally incompetent. Video film will be made of certain teachers' lessons and these will then be shown during the Eurovision Song Contest, so that the international juries can vote on them. Anyone getting 'nul points' will subsequently be dealt with through one of two experimental treatments.

Budget

Video camera	£1,000
Rifle	£250
Bullets	£250
Coffee	£250
Arsenic	£250

Dr H Crippen, Deputy Head (staff development), Hemlock Comprehensive School.

2 May 1997

Learn a lesson from Blackburn Rovers

So you want to climb up the league tables? Well that is precisely what every football club would love to do. Like Mount Everest, league tables are there to be climbed. Nobody wants to tumble down them. Here are ten hot tips for soaraway success.

Tip 1 *Start at the bottom*
Too many schools make the mistake of starting half way up, or worse, commencing their campaign at the very top of the league. This is a grave tactical error, as you will never get on to Ofsted's list of 'most improved schools'. Make sure everyone gets a lousy grade one year, ride out the flak, and you can then sit back and enjoy years of success as you claw your way off the bottom rung.

Tip 2 *Move your school*
There are certain areas that always do well in league tables, so smart schools will simply uproot themselves and move there. Among the best known league toppers are the Isles of Scilly. I recommend the Scillies. It is a pleasant place to live, and there are no major crime or pollution problems. Get your school towed out there and then simply moor it near a nice beach.

Tip 3 *The Blackburn Rovers strategy*
One of the best known success stories in football is that of Blackburn Rovers who acquired a wealthy patron, bought expensive players, and moved quickly from lower league obscurity to the championship of the Premier League. Find a multi-millionaire and then simply offer £1,000 scholarships to clever children. If anyone objects, simply call it 'parental choice'. Lots of other dubious policies have been sold under this label.

Tip 4 *Fire the manager*
The most common tactic in football is to sack the club manager when all is not going well. The chairman of the school's gover-

nors should call a press conference and announce, 'I have every confidence in the head teacher ... fine figure ... salt of the earth ... position assured ... no question of job not being safe ...' etc. The following week the head is pensioned off.

Tip 5 *Improve the gene pool*
It is well known that genetics plays a significant role in school achievement. Rewrite your school prospectus to state your policies clearly, like 'Stupid parents should apply elsewhere', or better still, 'Got a degree? No? Well get lost, thicko!'. The subtle approach is always best.

Tip 6 *Win the lottery*
Money may not be everything, but lack of resources can be a real problem. A quarter of primary schools spend less than £5 per pupil each year on books, and a half spend £10 or less. That barely purchases a decent book. Buy lottery tickets with your book fund. Think of the maths you can do instead (number, probability).

Tip 7 *Go private*
Private schools are supposed to get better results than state schools. They spend several times the amount that state schools spend on books. As social class and school achievement are highly correlated, simply announce that in future you will be charging £5,000 a year in fees. Call it 'parental choice' again.

Tip 8 *Get drunk*
Buy bottles of cheap supermarket plonk and get all the staff drunk. This won't actually change your school's league position, but the table will gradually go out of focus, so the staff will not be able to see, nor indeed care, where they are in the league. 'Parental choice' freaks invite parents to the Bacchanalian rites, for a fee.

Tip 9 *Get sponsorship*
All the best football teams are sponsored nowadays, so sign yourself up with the local dog food or spigot company. If there isn't one, then try the local bookmaker. It will make no difference to your league table position, but you might get a decent tip for the Derby.

Tip 10 *Draw up your own league*
The last tip is only for the desperate. There are strong arguments for adjusting raw league tables to take into account
various factors like prior achievement, or social background. So
if all else fails, then simply create your own league table of
schools with your outfit at the top. Tell everyone that it is a
'value added' table, and that you have used multiple regression.
No-one will have the faintest idea what you are talking about.
Make sure, by the way, that you say 'multiple regression', not
'multiple orgasm', as they are quite different, though for
statisticians they can be similar.

9 May 1997

Chapter 2
Wring out the old

Yippee! They're out, but the challenge is on

It was sad that the general election ended so badly for the outgoing government. No, that's not quite what I'm trying to say, let me rephrase it. It was a pity they lost so many seats. No, that's still not right. Let me try again.

Whoopee, whoopee, whoopee! Yoicks, tally ho, wowee! Thanks a million! Hip hip hooray! Oh what a wonderful morning! Yes yes yes, at last, at long last! Don't ring us we'll ring you. Bloody brilliant! On your bikes! Zippedy doo dah!

Yes, I think that is a bit closer to the feelings of the thousands of bleary eyed drunken teachers arrested for cartwheeling down the middle of the road all the way to their school at 5 a.m. on Friday May 2nd. Few tears were shed for a contemptuous government that had alienated most members of the major professions by treating them as if they were nothing more than self-interested serfs.

There are several elements of the last few years that should now be consigned to the refuse bin of history. Goodbye education ministers Simon Snakeoil, Cecil Clueless, Henry Halfbrain, Ralph Rightoffthewall and that hapless crew of actual and would-be right wingers who peddled their daft dogma. Farewell to those politicians who rubbished teachers remorselessly, irrespective of whether examination pass rates went up or down.

Enough of the past. As we approach the 21st century there are several challenges facing schools if we are to prepare children for what is likely to be a much more demanding lifestyle that that experienced by their parents and grandparents, both in work and in home and family life. Five issues in particular need to be given special thought.

Top of these is improving the achievements of boys. I have written elsewhere in the *TES* about this, so I shall not go into the detail here, but boys now lag behind girls at every stage of their education, particularly in language activities, like reading in the primary school and GCSE English in the secondary school.

Second, we must make sure we get the national curriculum right for the 21st century. The present version is due to expire in the year 2000, so the next one really will be a curriculum for the millennium. The consultation process starts next month and I would advise all teachers and heads to get involved in discussions whenever opportunities arise. There is a tremendous amount of professional experience of teaching a national curriculum now available, and it must be drawn upon.

The present timetable is that in April 1998 ministers will be asked if they want to change the national curriculum. If there are to be changes, then these will be worked out between summer 1998 and summer 1999. There should be a full school year thereafter, from the summer of 1999, during which primary and secondary schools will know exactly what they have to teach in September 2000, when key stages 1, 2 and 3 are scheduled to start, and September 2001, when key stage 4 begins.

I hope that Curriculum 2000 will be seen not just as a set of subjects, but as something fuller that prepares young people for what should be a long and fruitful life, since many of them will live to be ninety, a hundred, or more. Perhaps we can learn from experience last time that it is folly to over-prescribe the fine detail of what schools should do.

A third issue is the continuing mess in the education of pupils beyond the age of 16. It must be time to create a genuine equivalence of status between so-called academic and vocational courses and clarify the numerous pathways through what has rightly been called the 'post-16 jungle'. Students and their parents are completely baffled by the variety, standing, and particularly by the terminology of this infinite network of courses, modules and options. Bring out the flamethrower.

The fourth issue is one that is well understood by parents and teachers alike, that is the parlous state of our educational buildings. Schools in cities and in rural areas, colleges of further education, many universities, are having to use buildings that are a disgrace. Back in Victorian times the three decker schools were a model to pupils who lived in squalor at home. With electricity, heating and running water, they appeared as palaces to the children whose homes were often slums.

Now the opposite is the case. Many children live in houses that are in far better repair than some of our ancient pre-war (which war?) schools, with their dry rot and leaking roofs, and our 1960s concrete mausoleums, with their wet rot and leaking roofs. We need a major national effort to make school buildings models of a better future, not relics of an ancient past.

The fifth issue is the morale of the teaching profession. I started teaching in the 1960s, though I have no great nostalgia for that period, as there were some complete crackpots and fraudsters around. Nevertheless, I would love to recapture the spirit of adventure and excitement about education generated by Alec Clegg in what used to be called the West Riding of Yorkshire, and by the many heads and teachers who felt willing to have a go at something, without the uneasy feeling that they were probably breaking the law.

David Blunkett took an important step in writing to schools saying that he wanted a partnership. It is impossible to run thousands of primary and secondary schools without the support of the people who work in them. Teaching is a profession whose members came into it, in the main, because they wanted to improve the lot of future generations.

Alas, if only Simon Snakeoil, Cecil Clueless, Henry Halfbrain and Ralph Rightoffthewall had realised that 'Welcome aboard, friend', is a better way of achieving genuine partnership than 'On your knees, scumbag'. But that is in the past. The future beckons.

16 May 1997

Cars and shades as the language of lifestyle

Lifestyle. That's what it is all about apparently. We poor saps who flog away working in education have got it wrong. Education, education, education is nowhere near the top of people's priorities. I have it on good authority from a man I met who works in advertising and public relations that 'lifestyle' is what turns the British public on.

When you and I buy a book, a pair of sunglasses, a car, or a chargrilled chicken, mango and pineapple dinner for one, are we in fact purchasing these actual objects? No we are not. According to my advertising chum we are actually selecting a lifestyle, and that is what the decision to purchase is all about.

The advertising and public relations industry spends a fortune trying to find out about people's actual and preferred lifestyles. The outcome of this assiduous enquiry is a proliferation of adverts that are often more about people's dreams and aspirations than about the actual products. Look through any set of adverts and you will see this current orthodoxy shining through.

One book club ad stresses the friends your children will make if they read the right books. You thought that sunglasses were what you wore to keep the sun out of your eyes? Poor fool you then. Expensive sunglasses are for sad people who believe that they will bring success with the opposite sex, though quite how a piece of twisted metal and tinted glass can compensate for an inadequate personality and halitosis is beyond me.

Car ads suggest not only power and control, but being abroad, somewhere on the Mediterranean, or in the mountains. The writers of these minor literary masterpieces have conveniently forgotten traffic jams to Dover, evil cross channel ferry fish and chips, lorry drivers blockading the port on the other side and the ludicrous price of motorway tolls.

Advertisers' obsession with lifestyles have led to a whole new genre of newspaper supplement. Weekend newspapers in particular have so many pretentious lifestyle supplements it is quite an art to find the news or the particular bits you want. Indeed, the *Times Educational Supplement* has its own batch of pullouts. Only a lifestyle supplement is missing – until today, that is.......

ElbowPatch
The new-look TES lifestyle supplement
IN THIS ISSUE

Page 1 *A welcome to all readers*
Fiona Fluffy gives the lowdown on the brand new all-singing all-dancing TES lifestyle supplement for tired teachers.

Page 3 *Nifty Ned*
This week's page 3 pinup, Ned Nock, 35 year old design and technology teacher from Upper Swinesville Comprehensive, shows how to pierce your nipple safely with a Black and Decker, and then make your very own designer nipple rings out of old national curriculum files.

Page 5 *Pass the Rennies*
Our school meals special. A top French chef samples school dinners and awards from one to three Rennies for inedibility and up to five spittoons for school dining room ambience. In part two Dr Crippen, our resident lifestyle doctor, recommends a range of natural indigestion remedies for those who had to jump up too quickly to mark the thirty books that they collected in six weeks ago before 1-30.

Page 11 *Fit or bust*
Aerobics for teachers. Fitness guru Anna Rexic shows how you can do 'silent exercises' even during lessons! No more need to be unfit, as Anna demonstrates her three tiptop aerobic winners: (1) the 'eyeball', how to rotate your eyeballs so you will have iron class control and strengthen those neck muscles at the same time, (2) the 'leg-it', sprinting down the school drive at one minute past four and strengthening your leg muscles, (3) the 'cheeky', how to keep your spine in trim by clenching your bum cheeks together while writing on the blackboard.

Page 15 *Digging for gold*
Gardening expert Fred Fastbuck explains how you can set up a school garden, under the pretext of studying national curriculum science attainment target 2, 'Life processes and living things', and then sell the produce for profit without the head even finding out.

Page 17 *Hoots mon!*
Teachers send in their gaffes from Ofsted inspections. This week Elspeth Scattergood tells how she accidentally set the Registered Inspector's trousers on fire during her science lesson.

Page 19 *Where are they now?*
Our reporters track down former education ministers, with a few surprises. Sensational colour photographs of Kenneth Baker selling silk ties in Petticoat Lane, Kenneth Clarke mixing cocktails at the Dog and Duck, John Patten selling Big Issue, and Gillian Shephard gogo dancing in a Norfolk night club.

Page 23 *Motoring notebook*
How to fill the holes in the bodywork of your W-registered Escort with fibreglass and pulped national curriculum tickboxes.

Page 27 *Fashion*
Ball point pen leaked into your pocket? Don't panic. A top French couturier demonstrates how you can make the most horrible ink stain look like a natural part of the design, and also how you can then use the leaky pen to decorate your fading Hush Puppies so they look like trendy new ones.

Page 31 *Short and sharp*
Travel How a camping holiday in Doncaster can cost less than 50p a day.

Stress The teacher who conquered stress by sleeping through her lessons.

Competition Win Chris Woodhead's glasses, so you too can look hard, by completing the limerick, 'There was an inspector called Pitt, ...'.

30 May 1997

Success to the Woodlouse initiative

So can Chris Woodhead and Tim Brighouse actually work together? This was the question every journalist was asking when they were made joint vice-chairmen of the same committee, presumably to be known as the Brighead committee, or the Woodhouse committee. I knew something must be happening in the woodshed.

It all reminded me of a football coaching course I went on a few years ago. The old lag taking it was a well known centre half, notorious for his ferocious tackling. When I made a feeble challenge on the player I was marking he took me on one side. 'Look son', he said, 'you've got to let him know you're there. The first time he gets the ball, just drag your boot down his leg. When he's got six stud marks running down the back of his calf, he'll know you're there all right'.

Could Tim Brighouse's role, therefore, be that of 'tight marker'? Would he have to follow Woodhead around the pitch, studs upwards? If so, it will be a tricky assignment.

The more interesting question was whether or not opposites can work together. Looking back through history, for example, would Genghis Khan and St Francis of Assisi, those two contemporaries of the late 12th and early 13th centuries, who never actually met, have forged a harmonious partnership? 'Genghis, my old mate, how are the animals getting on?'. 'Er, actually I've eaten them all'. Maybe not.

On the other hand, the two cartoon characters Tom and Jerry sometimes make up. Unfortunately their exaggerated politeness signals that peace will not last very long. It is usually the wicked Tom who reneges on the tryst, with Jerry soon back in the frying pan.

When asked by a BBC interviewer how different Tim Brighouse and Chris Woodhead were, I resorted to the cliché 'like chalk and cheese'. I wondered afterwards if I might have upset any cheeses listening. Was Wooders an over-ripe gorgonzola or just a lump of hard cheddar? Or maybe a piece of Emmenthaler, the cheese with the hole in the middle.

Much of the press coverage got it wrong. Teachers did not like the Chief Inspector because he had criticised them, was a common theme. This is nonsense. It is quite true that Woodhead likes to portray himself as the courageous mountaineer, fearlessly taking on Miss Periwinkle of Year 2, but the reasons for his unpopularity are more complex.

Criticism of the profession has little to do with it. After all, the very same heads who supported strong action against incompetent teachers at their annual conference went on to vote unanimously that they had no confidence in Wooders. Getting a room full of heads to agree on anything, other than the need to pick up litter, is a remarkable achievement. If nothing else he has united the profession.

Back in 1979 and 1980 there were two large scale surveys by Her Majesty's Inspectorate of primary and secondary schools. The primary survey stated that only one class in ten was getting a decent science programme, that there was little experimental work and that nature study was commonplace, but physical science topics were rare.

Did the teaching profession riot at the revelation that there was too much tadpoles and sticky buds and not enough magnetism and electricity? Did anyone accuse Sheila Browne, the Chief Inspector of the day, of putting a spin on the evidence? Not at all.

The outcome of this devastating revelation was that many primary science courses were put on for teachers and lots of schools appointed a science co-ordinator. The national curriculum then incorporated more physical science topics. As a result the teaching of primary science is now infinitely better than it used to be. No Woodhead. No Ofsted. No rubbishing of primary teachers. Just a collective professional effort.

The reasons why Woodhead is not esteemed are threefold. First, he is known as someone who, having at one time been embarrassingly progressive, now portrays himself as an arch traditionalist. Anyone who works in a classroom is suspicious of such extreme conversions, as most practitioners make gradual and judicious changes.

Second, he has made the mistake of hobnobbing with right wingers. Indeed, the *Sunday Telegraph* described him as a right winger. Previous Chief Inspectors have kept their distance from political pressure groups. Woodhead not only produced a pamphlet for Sheila Lawlor's right wing think tank Politeia, but wrote it in the style of such pamphleteers. His close contacts with right wing newspapers are talked of freely by journalists. Ofsted pronouncements now lack credibility with the teaching profession.

Third, he portrays himself as the fearless champion of parents and children. This is seen as priggish by people who actually devote every day of their working lives to children and their families. It is as if he has sole lien on the public.

Nonetheless, despite these reservations, I do think it is important that ideological divisions should be put on one side and that people of all beliefs should work harmoniously together for the common good. I welcome the proposal that Tim Woodhead and Chris Brighouse should serve jointly on the Woodshed committee.

In the spirit of harmony and beneficence, therefore, I wish the new Woodlouse initiative every success. I am right behind it. So much so that I have been on a shopping expedition. I have decided to give both central players a present, to ensure a cracking start and a smooth path of progress for the committee.

My carefully chosen present to Chris Woodhead is a pair of radioactive boots, so he can be tracked down at the numerous lunches during which he gives the press his own unique version of events.

My special present to Tim Brighouse is a Geiger counter and a pair of football boots, the former so he can actually find Woodhead, the latter so he can let him know he is there.

13 June 1997

Economical with the classroom actualité

A few months ago a British conference organiser, hoping to arrange a great national conference on efficiency in business, telephoned an American who was reputed to be the world's leading expert on these matters. Would this transatlantic mega-genius be able to come to Britain to address an eager British business community?

'My fee will be £40,000 plus expenses', said the great man. The British organiser gulped and contemplated his modest budget. 'I'm sorry, but I'm afraid we couldn't possibly afford that', he replied, 'but just to satisfy my curiosity, can you tell me briefly what the gist of your message would have been on how we could improve our efficiency?'.

There was a pause. Then the global guru uttered just two words. (Normally these would retail at £20,000 each, but you can have them for nothing). 'Trust people', he said, and with that he put down the phone.

I found this true story irksome and cheering. I was a teeny bit narked, as I, like others, have been saying precisely the same thing for the last few years without being regarded as the world's leading guru on business efficiency. However, it was gratifying (a) that he mentioned people, rather than systems, and (b) that he advocated trusting them to use their intelligence, rather than accusing them of being incompetent, malevolent, or both.

When money is short there are few options. One is to make better use of what actually costs money, like people's time. The previous government's deep suspicion of the professions led to teachers, doctors, police officers and others being buried under mountains of paper. They were shackled instead of liberated. Bureaucracy replaced trust.

In my new role as world efficiency guru, I offer £40,000 tip number one. It is this. Buy (£10,000) yourself (£10,000) a (£10,000) shredder (£10,000). A shredder not only cuts useless paper into thin strips, but you can send it off to be recycled. Keep your shredder next to the mail rack. All junk mail and useless correspondence can be put straight back into circulation, without touching the digestive system of the reader.

The next step is to take a close look at all mission statements, written policies, school development plans and de-bullshit them. This would reduce many to a few paragraphs. It is here that lack of trust is at its sharpest. Deep suspicion of teachers means they are not trusted to do the job, unless they have written down that they want to 'raise standards' or 'deliver high kwality education'. It suggests a loaded Kalashnikov and sheets full of boxes are needed to secure commitment.

Of which school is this the mission statement? 'Our aim is to offer a first class education to every child. As the 21st century approaches, we are committed to raising the standards of all our pupils, so that they can face the rigours of an uncertain blah blah, glob glob, oodle noodle, flannel flannel, hot air, well meaning empty tosh, kwality kwality all the way, there's more of that where this came from, we're the Spice Girls and this is what we really really want ...'.

All schools write that they want the best. Are there any schools whose ambition is to lower standards? If so, shut them down. If you asked the lousiest school in the land to write a mission statement, would it not produce precisely the same pap as everyone else, whatever the reality? There is the language of mission statements and there is the actuality of classroom life, and sometimes the two are poles apart.

Be honest. Can you remember vast chunks of any written policy statement you have ever subscribed to? For ten points, no conferring, could you explain how your 1993 plan differed from your 1995 and 1997 plan? I have a good memory and I cannot even remember the ones I have written. The reality in schools is what people do, not what they write. Writing should be kept to a minimum.

My third world efficiency guru tip is this. Take (£8,000) a (£8,000) scythe (£8,000) to (£8,000) meetings (£8,000). Halve the number of meetings, halve the time of each one. Replace talk with action. Lack of trust by the last government led to an enormous increase in time spent on futile talk, as teachers tried to persuade real and imaginary snoops, and each other, that they were satisfying requirements.

There were fat meetings and thin ones; long meetings and, less often, short ones; angry, silly, jolly, funny, hilarious, anarchic, pompous and earnest meetings; planning, analysing, justifying, disputing, evaluating meetings; pre-inspection, during inspection and post-inspection meetings; therapeutic, repetitive, let-it-all-hang-out, sobbing sodding meetings. There were too many and they drained precious energy away from classroom work.

Just as writing should be confined to essential target setting, record keeping and evaluating, so meetings should be limited to analysing, planning, inspiring and enthusing. Windbags should agree to be gagged. Therapy seekers should take up yoga. Seasoned obstructionists should agree to number their comments, so they could just call out the numbers, instead of boring everyone into a coma – 'There's no call for it' (2a), 'That's the first I've heard of it' (4c), 'We did that in 1986' (7a), 'And it didn't work then' (7b).

Trust is a two way bargain. The price we pay for being trusted is that no-one must break the trust. Those who unwittingly do so should be offered help and support. If that is spurned then retribution will follow. It is actually a small price to pay for being trusted. The vast majority are allowed to get on with their teaching, not treated as potential criminals and buried under bureaucracy. That is what efficiency is – maximising the time spent on what is important, minimising the distractions. In summary: action, not words.

'So caper the paper and walk the talk'. That would have cost £5,000 a word from the American guru. Cheap at the price.

27 June 1997

Digits that add up to a plethora of piffle

There is a new exciting buzzword in the broadcast media. If you want to appear to be a 21st century, forefront-of-technology, state-of-the-art, trendy, progressive (steady on, you're talking to teachers, remember), streetwise technocrat, then one word must be on your lips. 'Digital'. That is the secret of life nowadays. Everything must be digital.

'It won't, of course, be a problem, once we go digital'. 'Oh yes. In the digital age, anything will be possible'. You get the hang of it? Every so often, until the rest rumble it, you alone can pretend to solve the very core of humanity's problems with a single word that will turn muck into gold. 'Digital' is today's version of the philosopher's stone.

In reality, all that 'digital' means is that radio or television signals are turned into a string of numbers. Since these numbers occupy a much narrower bit of the airwaves than conventional signals, and will not corrupt so easily in the transmission, you can create more radio or television channels.

One of the results that broadcasters get excited about, which is of particular interest to education, is the possibility of more specialist channels, devoted to one particular topic. These are very popular in the United States, as well as here. Avid watchers of such 'dedicated' channels can watch programmes entirely about 'furniture', or 'pets'.

Needless to say there is a price to pay for this sudden excess of airspace. Eager to fill the masses of time available on furniture or pet channels, programme makers produce a torrent of low budget, superficial piffle.

I once watched half an hour of unadulterated tripe on 'how to distress your wooden chairs'. No, you don't kick seven bells out of them. Apparently 'distressing' furniture is a means of making it look old and battered and it is all the rage. You paint your chair and then rub some of the new paint off. It ends up looking like the sort of furniture we owned when I was a child. Since most of us have spent a lifetime trying to afford stuff that is fit to sit on, it seems perverse, to say the least, to go out of your way to make it look tatty.

If that doesn't seize your imagination, then try the pet channel. There you will be able to learn a whole new array of skills, like how to cast your pet's horoscope. ('You will meet a tall dark guinea pig'?). I heard of one American fan of such programmes who found she had rats in her loft. She called in a 'rat psychologist' who came in to reason with them. What on earth did he say? 'Now look here, chaps. Let's talk about this like mature adult rodents...'? Surely not.

All of this made me wonder whether, in the digital age, the schedule for a dedicated channel for teachers might look something like this.

TEACHERS' CHANNEL
7.00am **Thought For The Day** Elspeth Scattergood tells how getting a grade 7 on a school inspection changed her life. Live from Holloway.

7.30 **Morning Service** Hymns include 'For Those In Peril', played by the prize-winning brass band of the John Major Rest Home for early retired teachers, sung by Johnny Patten and the Brimstones.

8.00 Close Down Until After School

4.00pm **Thank God They've Gone Home** Arnold Oldlag offers relaxation techniques for when lessons are over, and gives tips on how looking busy and harassed can help you avoid being asked to run an after-school club.

5.00 **Teacher's Pet** Senior Inspector Mike Tomlinson explains which members of the simian family he had in mind when he said he didn't give a monkey's toss about teachers.

6.00 **Dad's Army** Another episode of this popular comedy series in which Corporal Jones becomes a lay inspector and rushes into school staffrooms shouting, 'Don't panic!'.

6.30 **Masterchef** Three school cooks battle it out to see who can make the thickest custard, the hardest carrots and the wateriest potatoes, and win the coveted 'Foodmangler of the Year' title.

7.30 **The Teletubbies** Five writers of National Vocational Qualifications frolic round talking in a language that no-one can understand.

8.00 **Only Fools And Horses** The Teacher Training Agency hires Del Boy, Rodney and Grandad to deal with the teacher recruitment crisis.

8.30 **Distress Your Head** Top furniture expert Chris Wooden-top shows how wood ageing techniques can be used to make brand new head teachers look genuinely old.

9.00 **Masterteach Final 1997** Magnus Magnusson sits four primary teachers in the famous black chair. This week's specialist topics include: 'The invaders and settlers, from the beginning of time to the last busload of American tourists', 'Turning absolute crap into technology projects', and 'The Beacon Readers, 1901 to 1957'.

9.45 **Beavis and Butthead** Kenneth Clarke and Kenneth Baker debate who was the bigger prat when they were ministers.

10.15 **Late Film – Gone With The Wind** The story of how various teachers manage to secure early retirement by inventing imaginary ailments.

12.00 **Knackered** Last in the late-nite series 'Sex For The Debilated'.

11 July 1997

Conference call from the cowshed

Before you lock up the shop and head off for Benidorm or Bridlington, depending on where you are on the salary scale (Benidorm if you are at the bottom, Bridlington if you are at the top), do bear in mind that the September conference season is only a gnat's whisker away.

Conferences bring out hidden truths in the teaching profession. If you took a video camera along and filmed the participants, you could make a fortune in blackmail by threatening to show the secret life of the conference delegate.

Sober suited Mr Grimsdyke becomes hawaian-shirted Dave the Rave at the disco. Offer the normally discreet and tactful deputy head Mavis Scattergood a second glass of red wine during dinner, and she will bring out her stage whisper to tell you and the rest of the diners, and indeed anyone passing within half a mile of the conference venue, all the scandals that have befallen Swinesville School during the last thirty years.

Nowadays there is great business to be made out of conferences. Many hotels have been specially kitted out to cater for teachers' conferences in particular – cheap food, video projectors that don't work, rooms that get too hot or cold, plus other features for those missing their school.

There is often great fun to be had when several conferences take place at the same venue. I once arrived at a large hotel to find a businesslike lady rushing towards my car. 'Thank goodness you've come', she gasped, 'They're all waiting'. When I entered the room it was full of middle-aged businessmen surrounded by manufacturing company logos. I had to explain gently that I was not the person they were expecting to talk about the aerodynamics of the ball bearing or whatever.

A few weeks ago I was lecturing to an audience of head teachers. In the room next door there was another conference of people who sell anti-depressant drugs. The possibilities were endless. Couldn't the two get together and gratify each other? The heads could make bulk purchases of happy pills, while the tablet sellers could sit in on education sessions to discover why their business was doing so well.

Whenever a conference gets boring one way of pepping it up is to play the game 'Who does what?'. This is especially good fun when there are heads, teachers, education officials, governors, parents and politicians present. You try to guess which delegate is in which category. Then you check their badges to see if you were right.

There are certain guidelines here. The delegates picking up litter and chuntering are head teachers, that much is easy. The harassed looking members could be almost anybody. The parents are the people who appear even more relieved to be away from children than the teachers do. Office for Standards in Education inspectors are the ones who go around looking hunted and furtive, pretending to be the window cleaner. Her Majesty's inspectors are cheerful and laughing, telling everyone they are HMI, not Ofsted.

It is very easy to make monumental blunders on these occasions. A colleague and I once entered a room full of people in the university where I work. We had been told that there were many foreign dignitaries present, ambassadors even. Most spoke excellent English, but some were more hesitant, so we were to speak slowly and distinctly.

My colleague rushed over solicitously to a lady in a smart black dress standing on her own by the door. 'Good evening', he beamed, enunciating his words clearly, 'I'm Professor Scroggins and I work here at the university'. 'Nice to meet you', she replied. 'I'm the waitress. Do you want white wine or red?'.

There are numerous hazards if you are invited to lecture at a conference. Should your lecture be last in the programme, everyone else will have covered the ground three times already. If you lecture first, then all the other speakers will complain that you have drained their own topic dry. When I am on last I always check with the organiser to see what other people have said. 'Can't remember a thing', is the most common reply.

Another pitfall is the introduction. Most chairmen are well briefed, but some get it wrong. 'Our speaker today was born in Leeds', one began. ('Sheffield', I hissed, remembering that my father in law always claimed that people in Leeds never got washed.) 'He teaches at Essex University'. ('Exeter', I muttered). 'And he is a well known progressive'. ('Arch traditionalist, for goodness' sake. Do you want me to lose my job?').

One of my favourite introductions occurred when I went to Norway. 'We are delighted that Professor Wragg is able to open our conference', the chairman began, 'because Professor Hirst couldn't come and neither could Professor Peters'. Another chairman told the audience he was relieved I had agreed to lecture because most people were busy at that time of the year.

Then there is the problem of the venue. I have lectured in some toilets in my time, but the other week I had to address 200 teachers in what used to be a cattle shed, an irony that did not escape the audience.

Next door to the screened off area was an exhibition and also two other 'lecture rooms', a loose term meaning, in this case, 'an area of shed surrounded by a few low-rise screens'. The sound echoed round and round, bouncing up and down off the tin roof, fusing in with the neighbouring distractions. It all sounded like a badly mixed 1960s rock album.

So as the last register calls of July are logged in, as the school doors are locked for August, as the head picks up the last stray sweet wrapper in the playground, the consolation is that only six weeks from now September will be here. Then it will all start up again with a jolly good conference in the cowshed. Have a good Summer.

25 July 1997

For Alan Shearer, read Tinky Winky

August is known as the silly season. This is largely because schools are shut and journalists feel they can mess about while their former teachers are away.

'What on earth do you think you are doing, writing all that rubbish? You can do better than that. Now sit up straight, get a clean sheet of paper and start again. Write something sensible. Nothing silly. And make sure it's in your neatest handwriting'.

'Sorry Miss'.

The fuss about the BBC Teletubbies series is a prime example. For anyone who was out of the country in late August, let me explain that the Teletubbies are four rotund furry puppets, called Tinky Winky, Dipsy, Po and Laa Laa, who have television sets in their midriffs and who talk a funny language.

Instead of saying 'hello', they say 'haro' to each other. There, I knew you would be shocked. Apparently 'pundits' have claimed that this will ruin children's language for the rest of their life. 'Haro, Your Majesty', the Prime Minister of the day will say to some foreign dignitary in the year 2050, and World War 5 will break out.

Anyone who believes that most children cannot distinguish harmless nonsense words from good sense does not understand them. Many create their own 'in' language with friends or family anyway. Understanding a 'secret' code, even if it is known to millions of others, is part of the fun of being a child.

In any case, nonsense language is a central feature of the human race. When one of the Teletubbies says, 'Tinky Winky biddle boddle', he is simply preparing children who may in future want to join the teaching profession. One day they will be able to understand the language of National Vocational Qualifications, or the literature on kwality in education.

Unless, of course, the critics are right. Maybe the compilers of NVQs watched Bill and Ben the flowerpot men when they were young. That could explain why they write in their literature, 'The underpinning knowledge/understanding – ooh, flubbalubba – and the range statements – ooh flubbalub-balubba – as well as the performance criteria – ooh flubbalub-balubbaloo ...'.

Perhaps the kwality fetishists were raised on the Clangers, those little creatures who whistled and cooed their way through children's television programmes. 'Quality assurance is best delivered when the – whoooo whooooooooooooo ...'. It all begins to make sense now.

I was still mortified to hear that the Teletubbies were going to be made sensible and grown up. Anna Home, head of children's programming at the BBC, said: 'It may be there is a need to get into more traditional speech. There may be some modifications and we may hear some more adult language'.

More adult language? No, steady on Anna, don't do it. Ride the criticisms. Grown-up speech is not all it's cracked up to be.

'I say, Tinky Winky, have you been delivered of most of the programmes of learning and completed the attainment targets of Key Stage 1?'. 'No, Laa Laa. But I have fulfilled all the desirable learning outcomes of the pre-school phase of education'. Biddle boddle, Anna. Keep the Teletubbies childlike.

A German television executive then stated that they would not be shown on German television as they were too scary, saying: 'These are like spacemen. I think they will frighten our children'. Perhaps the only chance we have of winning next year's world cup is to pick Tinky Winky, Dipsy, Po and Laa Laa as the back four of the England football team, if they scare the pants off foreigners.

No silly season would be complete without at least one story that sounds daft, but turns out to be true. The Office for Standards in Education, the spiritual home of the Teletubbies, can usually be relied upon to provide one or two of these and this summer was no exception.

The best was an announcement from Tinky Winky Wood-head about the grading system for teachers when watched by inspectors. You may recall that teachers used to be placed on a five point scale. Last year this was changed to a seven point scale. In future it will be a three point scale.

If you are wondering when you last saw many rapid changes of mind and policy in such a short space of time, then it was back in 1991. Between May and September that year, the science national curriculum had first seventeen, then five and eventually four attainment targets. I am trying to recall who was in a very senior post at the National Curriculum Council in those vacillating times. Ah yes. Haro again, Tinky Winky Woodhead.

All Ofsted inspectors will in future dress as Teletubbies and rate teachers on the new rigorous three point scale. Grade 1 will mean 'Haro teacher. Dipsy thinks you are brilliant, but occasionally crap'. Grade 2 indicates 'Laa Laa says you are good, but sometimes crap', and grade 3 will mean 'Tinky Winky says you are biddle boddle crap'. Anyone suggesting there is a hidden agenda will have a television inserted into his midriff.

Another belter in late August was a review of school inspection reports by Ofsted itself. Apparently some of these contain the very same mistakes that inspectors are supposed to criticise in children's writing. There were grammatical, syntactical, spelling and punctuation errors. Worse, a number of suspect judgments were highlighted, like the inspectors who said teaching was 'satisfactory overall', when 43% of it was rated unsatisfactory or poor.

Stunning comments were cited, such as the startling conclusion 'Where teaching is good, pupils are challenged'. Confucius could not have put it better. I would rank that alongside some of the great human insights of the age, like 'When it rains, you might get wet', or 'If it's Friday today, yesterday must have been Thursday'.

Haro haro haro. This is pure biddle boddle flubbalubba, Tinky Winky.

5 September 1997

Warning: Literacy can damage relationships with your children

I'll tell you what. Why don't I hear you read, Jason.

Oh, mum, do I have to?

Miss Scattergood says it will help the school's literacy drive and it should do your reading a bit of good as well. After all, Jason, now that you're six you should soon be taking these SAT thingies, or whatever they're called, so it'll be good practice.

What's a SAT, mum?

It's a test you have to do when you're seven.

And what's a literacy drive? Is it like that place by the house where dad parks his car?

No, Jason. That's the drive that comes up to our garage. A literacy drive is, well, it'll teach you a lot of new words, like, er...

Like that drive that dad said was bloody useless when he came back from golf.

No that was his golf shot, and don't you use language like that in this house.

But you said the school wanted a drive so I could learn a lot of new words.

No, Jason. You see, all the children in Miss Scattergood's class have to do a reading test at the end of the year when they're all seven.

I'm seven in October. Can I do it then? I want to do it before Darren Clark. He's not seven till June, so he's just a big baby.

Now don't you start falling out with Darren Clark again. You all do the test on the same day next May, and ...

That's not fair. Darren's younger than me. I should do it first.

Well never mind that. Now what was I saying? Ah yes. If I hear you read then Miss Scattergood says it will help you do better and the school will move up the league.

The league. Oo goodie. Can we play football then? Can we play Man United?

No, it's nothing to do with football. Miss Scattergood says that when you read to me I'll be more patient, because I'm your mum and I've only got one child, while she's got 34.

Miss Scattergood shouts a lot.

Well I won't need to shout, because I'll only be hearing you read. Now let's look at this book Miss Scattergood has sent home, 'Little Twinky meets the Big Pink Fairy'.

It's boring. I don't want to read it. I hate that Little Twinky. He's a wally.

Well I think it looks a very nice book.

It's just boring. Is there a book called 'Little Twinky gets eaten by a killer shark?'

Now don't be silly Jason. Let's read this nice book and I am sure it will help the school's literacy drive a lot. Look I'll start, 'Hello Big Pink Fairy', said Little Twinky. 'Hello jolly nice Little Twinky', said the Big Pink Fairy'. Go on. You read the next bit.

I don't want to. It's a stupid story.

Well read it anyway. Look it's easy. 'Do you want some yummy yummy bread and jam in your tummy wummy?', asked the Big Pink Fairy ...

'No I want some jilly jelly in my silly belly', said Little Twinky ...

It doesn't say that at all. Jason. Now stop being stupid and read the next bit properly.

You said you wouldn't shout at me because you were my mum. Miss Scattergood shouts at us all the time.

I AM NOT .... I am not shouting. Now I want you to try your best. We must help the school's literacy drive. Your head teacher will get cross if I don't hear you read, and the Government will put me in prison. Read the next page and you can have some sweeties.

Can I have some Star Wars figures instead?

No they're too expensive. All right then, there's no need to cry. If you read a whole page you can have a Star Wars figure.

If I read two pages can I have an intergalactic space station as well?

No they cost fifteen pounds. All right, all right, stop crying and read two pages and you can have the intergalactic space station. I don't know how Miss Scattergood copes with 34 of you. I find it bad enough with one.

She shouts a lot.

Just read the book.

Little Twinky – er – went – with – the – Big – Pink – Fairy – to – the – er – er – lack ...

To the lake. That says 'lake', not 'lack'. For goodness' sake. CAN'T YOU READ?

You're shouting, just like Miss Scattergood. So he pushed the Big Pink Fairy into the lake and she was gobbled up by killer sharks.

IT DOESN'T SAY THAT. I AM NOT SHOUTING. NOW JUST READ THE BLOODY BOOK PROPERLY. AND SIT UP STRAIGHT JASON ROBBINS, OR YOU CAN STAY IN ....

12 September 1997

Too hot to trot in the discipline dance

'Darren Rowbottom!'

Only teachers can speak those two words in 199 different voices and intonations, covering menace, intrigue, anticipation, congratulation, curiosity. Really versatile teachers can even signal the kind of moral outrage normally reserved for severe cases of grievous bodily harm, and that just for dropping a sweet paper.

In various research projects I have analysed several thousand lessons. I have also taught 'difficult' primary and secondary classes. I thought I was a dab hand at keeping order, but I seem to have missed a trick or two, judging by one local authority course on the subject.

Apparently teachers were given advice on discipline, which stated: 'You can use long, slow, sweeping gazes: e.g. looking out of the window, or looking dreamily at a display, or sweeping your eyes across the children with a gentle smile. Be still and use slow and soft hand signals to hush or calm behaviour that's out of sync with the tone of the movement'.

Now I have to confess I have not actually given such techniques a serious try. This must be because I hate dancing. It all sounds too much like the 'slow waltz', which I learned to detest when, at the age of seventeen, I used to go along to the local dance academy to learn what was euphemistically called 'ballroom dancing'.

Beetroot faced teenage lads were dragged along the parquet floor, feet all over the place, muttering in unison, 'Left two three, right two three, round two three, back two three'. Callow youths like us had had little arts education at the time, beyond art and music lessons and an avid read of Charles Atlas's 'You Too Can Have A Body Like Mine'.

Our tutors were taffeta-encased pink (keen apprentice) and blue (old bag) Barbie dolls. As we clumsily demolished a slow waltz, lovingly played by Mantovani's tumbling strings, one of the blue tulled Gauleiters would call out hopefully, 'Try to float like a dream'. We members of the acne brigade were scarred for life by the slow waltz trauma.

So when it comes to discipline, I can only 'look dreamily out of the window', or 'sweep my eyes across the children with a gentle smile' to the accompaniment of Mantovani, and even then I'm likely to be 'out of sync with the tone of the movement'.

Nor was some of the other advice in the same teachers' course much use to me. 'Draw happy faces on the blackboard'. Er, I don't think so. Improve achievement by 'dropping marbles in a jar' was another hot tip. This arresting trick has not yet penetrated my repertoire, I am ashamed to admit, but I ought to give it a proper trial.

'Right then (plink). Pay attention (plink). Okay (plink), settle down Year 9 (plink). I want to improve your achievement (plink plink). Darren Rowbottom! (plink plink plink). Put that fire out NOW! (plink plink plink plink plink plink)'.

The difficulty with the 'bag of tricks' approach to discipline is that it addresses symptoms instead of causes. A teacher with weak control could be advised to strip naked, stand in the waste paper basket and sing Ravel's Bolero in a high-pitched wail. This might silence an unruly class for a second, but it would not cure problems of poor personal relationships or inappropriate work, even if the teacher caught pneumonia.

Skilful classroom management, a far wider topic than 'discipline', underpins effective teaching. One American summary of several hundred research projects concluded that classroom practices were much more influential on pupils' learning than local or national policies and that, within the heading 'classroom practices', it was classroom management that seemed to bear most strongly on how well they achieved.

Our studies of classroom management show that most discipline problems, in primary and secondary schools, consist of noisy chatter or illicit movement. There is little 'serious' misbehaviour, barely two per cent of the incidents we analysed. In primary schools we found that 7-9 year olds were less well behaved than other age groups.

The problems often occur because of inappropriate work being set, or inconsistent application of rules. Unless these fundamental problems are addressed, there is little point in teachers learning a set of 'techniques' which simply give brief respite from the mayhem.

Approaches to classroom management reflect the context in which they occur. Some teachers are perfectly capable of managing idiosyncrasies, like 'looking dreamily at a display', which others would find comical or ineffective.

One teacher I knew used to shout 'Fire!' from time to time when he wanted complete silence. He was a much beloved character, so he got away with it. Anyone else would have been carted off to the Kenneth Baker Rest Home.

Another teacher had an arresting way of coping with excited pupils getting changed after playing football, and not listening when he asked them to collect their valuables. 'Anyone claim these watches before I stamp on them?', he would call out. It worked every time.

Trying to make one teacher's idiosyncrasies work for everybody is not the way ahead. I for one shall continue to develop my own approaches. No dreamy waltzes, no gentle smiles. Not for me the Victor Sylvester or the Mona Lisa solution.

No marbles dropped into jars, as they might think I've lost mine if I did. No 'happy faces' drawn on the blackboard, since I usually score at age five on the Goodenough 'Draw a Man' test. I once drew my daughter a picture of a feather. She thought it was a sausage.

But play an old Mantovani record and I might just react to the tumbling strings. 'Right, two three. Listen, two three. Let's look dreamy, two three. Yawn, two three. Zzzzzzzzzz, two three. Who are those men in the white coats, two three? Why are you lacing me into that jacket with the straps, two three? Put me down you fools, two three'.

19 September 1997

Problems solved at the drop of a hat

A few years ago the clothing industry began to realise that fashions were changing. As the 'natural' look developed, people stopped wearing headgear. Some advertising executive, shrewdly deciding that an appeal to personal ambition might work, came up with the neat catchphrase 'If you want to get ahead, get a hat'.

The news story about the reluctance of many teachers to become heads of schools reminded me of this clever slogan. Applications for headships have plummeted, as deputies and senior teachers decided they would not touch one of the most important jobs in our society with two barge poles tied end to end. Unfilled vacancies have soared, and numerous schools began the year with an acting head teacher.

The advertising slogan for hats could be adapted for schools without leaders. For chairmen of governing bodies who want to be able to walk all over the new incumbent: 'If you want to get a head, get a mat'. To emphasise the ability to deal with pests of one kind or another: 'If you want to get a head, get a cat'.

The crisis cannot have been helped by a startling headline in the national press recently. It read: 'Head removed in surgery'. Curious to know whether this was the latest method of dealing with the leader of a failing school, I read on eagerly.

Had the poor beggar been forced to visit his GP to have his vitals severed? Had he perhaps clung so firmly to his desk, when they tried to fire him, that only a scalpel could prise him off? Did they give him an anaesthetic? Or was he made to write mission statements until his whole body turned numb and unfeeling?

The story had nothing to do with head teachers. Apparently a team of surgeons had succeeded, for the first time, in detaching someone's head and then reconnecting it. I realised immediately that this new surgical technique could solve several problems in educational leadership.

There has been a suggestion, from time to time, that money could be saved if two or more schools shared the same head teacher. Another idea was that heads who do well in school inspections might also have an oversight of other, less successful schools.

Up to now these proposals have been thought to be impractical – too much stress, not enough time, geographical distance, and so on. The new 'head removal' surgical technique solves everything at a single stroke, so to speak. The successful head teacher's bonce can simply be detached and put on a stick.

Remember when iced lollipops were called the 'drink on a stick'? Well this would be the 'head on a stick'. Brilliant. It will be named the 'Worzel Gummidge solution' after the beloved children's television scarecrow character who had a series of detachable heads on sticks, allowing him to assume different characters.

The school down the road is having a riot? No problem. Get an ambulance and rush Worzel's nut over in a crate. Then all you have to do is attach it to the body of the poor beggar who cannot cope. Easy.

The head-on-a-stick approach could have many other effective applications. Suppose the head is feeling jaded. Simply take a fresh Worzel out of the cupboard, dust it down, screw it on to the weary shoulders of Mr or Ms Knackered, pour a glass or two of Phyllosan ('fortifies the over-forties') down its throat, and all will be well.

There must be considerable commercial possibilities here for a financial killing. My new limited company will surely be a commercial blockbuster and our 1998 catalogue is already rolling off the presses. We at Rent-a-Head will be offering a series of versatile Worzels for schools with problems.

The 1998 range includes a number of exciting new screw-ins. I fully expect the Machiavelli to be a best seller, guaranteed to turn the most innocuous head teacher into a wily scheming manipulator. If you want to get a head, get a rat.

Is the head unable to persuade the governors? Rent-a-Head has the answer. Screw in our Dame Edith for the acting performance of the century, not a dry eye in the house. The Branson model will also be ideal for schools struggling financially. Heads who are clueless about raising extra cash will develop into brilliantly successful entrepreneurs.

Are assemblies boring? Worry not. The 1998 Spice Girls range offers a set of five detachable heads with five different attractive and vivacious personalities. Hymn practice need never again appear to drag. The Posh Spice model is aimed at working class heads wanting to improve their image.

Nor has school security been forgotten. Top of the range here is our Woodhead. This hand crafted Worzel is a bargain at £9.99, complete with short cropped wiry hair and severe glasses. Stick it on a pole by the front gate to keep out undesirables.

As an ambitious new company, Rent-a-Head will be extending into related fields. Any local authority with a dreary chief education officer will surely purchase our Brighouse, certain to inspire heads and teachers with fresh enthusiasm and ideas.

Our Pavarotti will also be a winner. It is not guaranteed to improve performance, but it enables the CEO to comment acidly to the chairman of the education committee on any lack of cash for schools with a quick burst of 'Your tiny hand is frozen'.

A few years ago someone suggested that people who had failed in industry might retrain as teachers and then become heads, as if inadequate management in one field would somehow, magically, become good management in another.

There may be a crisis in the recruitment of new heads, but desperate solutions would be the last straw. The message is clear: if you want to get a head, don't get a prat.

3 October 1997

Recruitment needs more than sweeteners

Remember those history book stories about the man with the horse and cart who went round the streets during the plague, ringing a bell and shouting, 'Bring out your dead'?

As the teacher recruitment crisis balloons at an alarming rate, I propose that he and his horse be brought back under a job creation scheme. Before long anyone not actually on a life support machine, and indeed a few who are, will have to be wheeled out.

Some recruitment wizard is no doubt planning to disinter a few deceased schoolies, drape them in gown and mortarboard (should please traditionalists), prop them up on a frame in front of a class, and switch on a video. The key question in interviews for teaching posts will soon be: 'Has the candidate got a pulse?'.

There have been several interesting news stories about the growing scarcity of teachers. One item said that, as the shortage of applicants for vacancies grows, some teachers are hand picking the schools to which they apply. Another newspaper account reported that millions of pounds will be spent to improve teachers' image, in order to find new recruits.

The shortages have been exacerbated by the massive departure of teachers in their fifties who quit earlier this year, just as the axe fell on early retirement schemes. Before long they will no doubt be invited to return. No-one should claim to be surprised by the crisis. The problem has been building up for all to see.

When I wrote to the DfEE some time back, pointing out that circumstances would soon produce the worst teacher shortage in recent memory, I received a soothing reply. The gist of it was: there is no impending crisis, but thanks for writing. Good doggie. Pat pat. Here's a biscuit. Now bog off back to your kennel. Well 'Woof woof' is all I can say.

The roof would have fallen in earlier but for the 'No vacancies' solution. When teachers left and were not replaced, class sizes simply went up. If a maths teacher departed and there was no money for a replacement, or no-one suitable applied, then some poor beggar, if necessary a historian with an abacus, was stuck in front of a maths class and told to get on with it. One way or another the 'vacancy' became a phantom.

My heart always sinks when I hear the 'improve the image' solution. The idea of spreading a thin layer of glistening, but opaque slime over something, in order to conceal the harsh reality underneath it, has been in vogue ever since Kenneth Baker made slimatology respectable. Unfortunately it addresses symptoms instead of causes.

Expensive newspaper adverts, presumably written in estate agent English, are a waste of money – 'Wanted desirable, much sought after candidates to teach tastefully appointed, select bijou reception class pupils'. Nor does there seem to be much attraction in direct exhortation through cinema and television adverts – 'Come and teach, you bastards'. Can't see it working.

Teaching is one of the most important jobs in our society. It took thousands of generations to discover that water consists of two atoms of hydrogen and one atom of oxygen. A teacher can transmit the information to the next generation in ten seconds. Without teachers society would slide irrevocably back into primitive squalor.

There would have been no need to resort to slimatology had teachers not been hammered so hard during the last few years. The job is intrinsically interesting and rewarding. Many of the best young people of their generation know that and are attracted by the profession. They would be happy to join it, if only the conditions and climate were better.

Small wonder that some teachers, basking in their scarcity, are reported to be hand picking their next job. Armed with league tables and other school data, these smart operators are said to be giving interviewing committees a hard time. I can just picture the scene....

'Ah, come in, Mr Jenkins. Do sit down. I'm the chairman of governors and we'd like to ask you a few questions about your application for the post of head of maths here at ...'

'I'll not take my coat off, as I might not be stopping too long. Now look here, er, Ramsbottom, isn't it? Well, some working class name or other. Let me just look at my checklist. Ah yes. I see the maths department was only described as 'generally sound' in your Ofsted report, so what's the form on that one, Ramsbottom?'

'I er, perhaps the head teacher can answer that, er, I think he's got the report in his ...'

'And while little sunbeam is collecting his thoughts, perhaps you could tell me why you're only sixth out of ten schools in the Swinesville league table. I'm not prepared to turn out for a second division side'.

'We had a bad intake that year. Honestly Mr Jenkins ...'

'Call me 'sir".

'Honestly, sir, we're doing our best in difficult circumstances'.

'And while we're on with it, Ramsbottom, do you do staff cars? A nice new Jaguar XJS would come in handy. Do I get BUPA membership? Private education for the kids? I certainly wouldn't want mine to attend a fleapit like this. What about time off? Do you mind if I skip Mondays and Fridays – never at my best then – and come in after ten o'clock and leave at two, so I can miss the rush hour?'

'Well, we are very short of maths teachers, sir, so you can have whatever you like...'

Dream on, Mr Jenkins, we are not quite there yet. But it will take more than honeyed words to solve the recruitment crisis. Never mind sliming over the problems. The reality is that most teachers love teaching, but not the aggravations that go with it nowadays. Remove those and new recruits would flock in.

17 October 1997

Come on down, Joe Targeteer

We obsessives love ticking off targets. (That's six words I've written already). Single figure, or two, three, four digit targets, let them all come. Tall thin, short fat, round, square, oblong or diamond-shaped targets, no matter. You set targets, we obsessives will meet them.

Take my daily run. Every morning, without fail, I go for a run. This morning I reached the first telephone box on my route after 400 strides. That was 400 exactly, by the way. You just have to pace it right. Sad, I know, but targets are there to be hit.

Tomorrow I will aim to reach the telephone box in 390 strides. This should bring me nicely to a precise 800 strides at the junction by the big white house.

I did once increase the target to the telephone box day by day, until I arrived there after only 299 strides. It was a monumental feat.

Having broken the 300 barrier, the only reason I stopped was because I was risking a double hernia, so I put it in my 'silly targets' mental file. Passers-by would stare in amazement at this demented kangaroo, bounding along in a track suit, muttering '256, 257, 258' through clenched teeth.

So when it comes to official literacy and numeracy goals for the next millennium, or the one after, for that matter, I'm your man. I know lots of like-minded obsessives, so I can also rustle up a whole team of Olympic standard targeteers for you, no problem. (That's 248 words up to now, nearly a quarter of my target already reached).

The trouble with setting national or local targets is that not everybody can be driven by them. People with high achievement motivation revel in trying to meet specific objectives. Others, however, are intimidated by them, and some are totally indifferent. Even target fanatics can be put off by goals that are beyond them.

If setting and meeting specific targets is to be a central feature of our effort to equip children as fully as possible for the complexities of life in the next century, then a good deal of thought must be given to the whole process.

In 1993, as part of the Birmingham Education Commission, Tim Brighouse and I worked into the early hours one night to devise a realistic scheme of target setting for the city of Birmingham. We came up with several features we thought were important.

First of all, schools had to be involved in the setting of their targets. If each school could improve on its previous best, this seemed a more realistic way of raising standards than merely imposing city-wide figures. If every school could in fact do better, then the city's overall performance would automatically improve.

Second, targets should be monitored, so that there was some accountability. A school with a greatly changed intake, for example, might have to set different targets compared with one where the type of pupil entry had not changed.

An important third point was made by an industrialist member of the Birmingham Education Commission. In industry and commerce, he commented, an overall commitment to improve production would be accompanied by an investment plan.

A fourth suggestion was that targets should not be confined to numeracy and literacy. Why should children not be entitled to learn to swim, play a musical instrument, go on a field trip, take part in a public performance, see a theatrical production, participate in an environmental project, help in the community as a good citizen?

Many of the proposals made were implemented. Birmingham schools did try to improve on their previous best and most succeeded. The city did invest more money in its schools. The result has been an impressive increase in children's test scores, the latest figures showing well above national average improvements.

In the Leverhulme Primary Project which I directed, we found an interesting range of practice in the setting and monitoring of targets. There were reservations as well as endorsements for the idea. Greatest enthusiasm seemed to come from schools that were setting and trying to meet their own targets.

As an overall strategy for raising children's achievement target setting is still unproven, despite some impressive circumstantial evidence from Birmingham. It clearly depends on how it is implemented. It can be a useful servant, but a cruel master.

Just imagine if it came to dominate our lives. Obsessives like me and my pal Joe Targeteer would love it. After Joe finishes his second wheaty thing for breakfast, not one bite more nor one bite less, with his precisely 200 millilitres of semi-skimmed milk, in just three minutes, he sets off for work.

Leaving home at his exactly predetermined hour, he drives the 3.87 miles (measured daily on the trip mileometer, having found the shortest route years ago) in a record time. Phew, good job the last set of lights were on green.

Joe Targeteer calls the register in under a minute, but only just, (damn Wolfram-Eschenbach and Zabkiewiech).

Then he hands out the 32 books he marked the evening before (another record time achieved, it used to take over 70 seconds, until last night, just 68 seconds each on average, but that's not including the time it took to pick up one book and put down another, which would have added another three seconds and pushed it over the 70 second mark – that's not cheating, honest, only fair play).

The children have done quite well. Seventeen exceeded their target of 250 words (thank goodness it's a majority, so Joe can now legitimately write in his neat little record book 'Most children met their target', even though Darren Rowbottom only wrote 'This is complete and utter garbage' 42 times).

If only the whole human race was constructed like Joe and me, I am sure our problems would be over. We targeteers will leap through fire to tick off our tasks.

So I'll just count up the words one more time ... 992, 993, 994, 995. Target achieved. Done. Another tick.

31 October 1997

Spicy Chris and Mel on a unicycle

I have been puzzling over a little mystery. What brings together three people: a former junior minister, a dyspeptic journalist and a much admired public figure? Is it perhaps the Spice Girls?

Everybody wants to be spicy nowadays. The astonishing success of the Spice Girls has brought with it a string of admirers. World celebrities, like Nelson Mandela and Prince Charles, were happy to be seen in their company and were soon labelled 'President Spice' and 'Prince Spice'.

You can see the appeal. Spice is a term for those aromatic vegetables, like pepper and nutmeg, that give additional flavour to food. The last few years have been dreary, so anything that perks us up is welcome. The Spice Girls concept is now synonymous with a sparky, no-nonsense approach to life.

I was inspired by the spicy five when I read George Walden's column in the *Sunday Times* a couple of weeks back. Now you may or may not remember old George. He was one of that production line of junior ministers under the last Government whose epitaph read, 'They came, they went'.

George Walden was, I thought, better than the rest of the droids. Theodore Thingy, Agatha Airhead and Henry Hoozhee had no idea. George was a cultured man who did have an idea. He only had one idea, and it wasn't a particularly brilliant idea, but at least he had one. George's idea was to spend public money on sending children to private schools.

The trouble with bestriding a single idea is that it is difficult to get anywhere on just one wheel. Riding the same unicycle over and over again can eventually make someone wobble round and round in a circle.

Anyway, the other weekend I was quietly reading George's familiar rant in the *Sunday Times* about the demise of the assisted places scheme, when I came to a bit where he described me as being 'the problem' in education because of my 'complacency' and 'old-world egalitarian instincts'.

Oo er, I mused, a bit saucy of George, but who cares about being hit on the head with a wet lettuce leaf? Then I thought, complacent eh? Guilty of complacency if you don't protest, guilty of it if you do. Well bugger it. He may be two wheels short of a tricycle, but why should we Spice Profs sit back and take that kind of tosh?

However, this is where the intriguing mystery began. I was soon deflected from penning a riposte in the *Sunday Times*, when I noticed the startling similarity in tone between old George's piece and a column written by Melanie Phillips in the *Observer* a few weeks earlier.

Melanie Phillips wrote a book last year. It was very well written, but people have been complaining about the errors and false precepts in it ever since. Teachers were accused of propagating 'the doctrine that no value or activity can be held to be any better or worse than any other'. I have still to meet a teacher who equates murder and charity, but I digress.

Consider the striking similarities between the two Sunday columns. Neither thinks much of schools and teachers. George Spice writes of 'the mediocrity of the whole system'; Mel Spice speaks of 'our education disaster'.

Both suggest that current education ministers are in conflict with each other. George claims it is 'old Labour' versus 'new Labour'. Mel claims that some ministers believe in raising standards, others in lowering them.

Like George, Mel also attacks me, I am relieved to say. I wouldn't want all my street credibility to evaporate if she agreed with me. Mel was beside herself because I am a member of an advisory quango.

The former junior minister's and the dyspeptic journalist's hearts clearly share a common beat. But why? What do George Spice and Mel Spice really really want? And where does the aforementioned greatly admired public figure come into the mystery?

Well, another common factor in this intriguing saga is that they both seem to regard Chris Woodhead's attacks on the teaching profession as a solution. George calls him 'that most intrepid of crusaders'. This leaves the obvious poser, however: if Woodhead is the answer, what on earth is the question?

This cosy threesome reminds me of a radio variety show when I was a child, which always ended with the song 'We three in Happidrome . . . Enoch, Ramsbottom and me'. They should meet for lunch.

The good news, Spice fans, is that I have found an article that Chris Woodhead wrote in this very newspaper in the 1970s, when he was an English teacher. It shows clearly that deep down he is not Stiletto Spice, but Soft Spice.

In a piece called 'No bells, no sanctions', he tells how he took his class to a residential writing school for a week. He even wrote a poem himself and was patted on the head by the tutor, with moving effect, as he describes.

'I was taken back 20 years to my miniature primary school desk, when Michael Baldwin, one of our two resident writers, said he liked my poem. This ridiculous but real need for re-assurance means that the personality of the writers who tutor the course is a crucial factor in how the week goes'.

Ironic indeed, but I must admit, I did wipe away a flood of tears as I thought of little Wooders, first in his grey flannel shorts in junior school, wide eyed and eager to please Mr Chalkie, and then later as an adult in suit and serious glasses, grateful for a crumb of approval for his poem.

14 November 1997

Who shall punish the punishers?

'You snivelling wretch. You curmudgeonly nincompoop. You creepy, useless, bankrupt little toad. You moaning, skiving, loafing, idling parasite. You cringing, whinging piece of yak dung. You ...'

Oops! Sorry about that. I was so taken with the proposal that head teachers of failing schools would be called in to see ministers if they failed to improve, I got carried away trying to envisage the scene, as hapless head met angry minister.

It raised the whole question of retribution and what should be done with people who fail to meet their obligations. There is a certain irony in those normally expected to administer reprimands, actually being sent away to receive some themselves.

The rules on the punishment of pupils are fairly clear. It must be what is called 'reasonable and moderate', administered in good faith, such as is usual in the school, and what a reasonable parent might expect to be given. So extra work is permissible, but thumbscrews and boiling in oil are not.

One major function of school sanctions is to terminate the behaviour that is disapproved and avoid reoffending. Some forms of punishment may not always achieve this.

When I started teaching we had a rota of teachers, each taking it in turn for a week to supervise pupils kept in at lunch time or after school. One of the old lags told me that he made detainees copy out chunks of Milton, on the grounds, mistaken I thought, that this would improve both their handwriting and knowledge of English literature.

During my week of duty I decided on a different approach. On Monday I asked all the junior criminals to devise an advertising campaign to sell fridges to Eskimos. On Tuesday I got them to plan a society where there would be no crime. By Wednesday the room was packed. Detention had become the most popular after-school club.

Teachers began to complain that pupils were misbehaving on purpose so they could be kept in after school. The old lag took me on one side, explaining that I must have got the wrong end of the stick and offering to lend me a class set of 'Paradise Lost'.

Sending failing heads to see the minister might have a similar effect. After all, the present crowd of ministers are a more interesting lot than some of their predecessors. It would have been a pleasure to be told off by Sir Keith Joseph, but being oiled to death by Kenneth Baker, bemused by John Patten, or to meet Kenneth Clarke, only to discover he did not know why you were there, would probably have had the most recalcitrant head begging to be let out.

In the absence of a rack nowadays, one minister could hold the head's legs and another grasp the head's arms. If the two of them then walk vigorously away from each other, the head would be stretched. People seeing an excessively tall head could then say, 'Hello. Been to see the ministers then?', which would be tough on some poor head who just happened to be six foot six anyway.

So will a day out in London and a ministerial wigging actually work? Only if it is related to other events. I can understand the frustration of people in charge, if every approach has failed. The desire to do something personally becomes overwhelming.

Schools will only improve, however, if the quality of teaching and learning within them gets better, and this needs action in the classroom. Local intervention will be necessary, with the emphasis on improving teachers' skills. I would make the improvement of teaching and learning the top priority for all heads, and shred the useless bureaucracy under which so many have become buried.

A second step would be to close down all local authority business units which require advisers to meet annual financial targets by travelling to schools, sometimes hundreds of miles away, to do inspections for the Office for Standards in Education.

This is a huge waste of local taxpayers' money. What kind of business or educational sense does it make to earn about £200 per day for sending a skilled adviser to inspect some distant outpost, well outside the region, when it probably costs the LEA £400 per day in wages and overheads? Meanwhile the LEA's own failing schools are crying out for on-the-spot help. Madness.

If retribution is still necessary, then there must be a sliding scale of punitive sanctions that would concentrate the mind of any unsuccessful head. In one Monty Python sketch you could actually pay someone to shout insults at you, so perhaps that sort of service could become a reality.

If the professional shouter fails, then the equivalent of Orwell's Room 101 could be a library packed with national curriculum and vocational qualification literature. Heads would be forced to read about performance criteria, range statements and flangified breezlebums until they hammered on the window and promised to reform.

Like those computer games, where you eventually have to do battle with the monsters to be found in the higher tiers of the Kingdom of Thargon, there could be a final stage. The sanctions would be ranked in order of awesomeness, culminating in the ultimate.

The top four punishments, guaranteed to rescue even the greatest lost cause, would start with, in fourth place, being put in charge of someone else's failing school. This might not be too bad, as you could always tell morning assembly the story about Robert the Bruce, without everyone groaning, 'Not that one again'.

In third place would be a week trying to teach national curriculum design and technology to a non-examination Year 10 class, followed by, in second place, having to explain 'competitive tendering' to a group of specially selected dim governors.

The ultimate sanction would be a conducted tour of Ofsted, followed by tea and scones with Woodhead. 'Paradise Regained', as Milton put it. They'd soon come off special measures.

28 November 1997

Hitlists, gremlins and a new song

Only three more Christmas celebrations before the millennium, so there is still time to have a rousing 20th century festivity, before the next hi-tech era arrives. For anyone who has run out of ideas for traditional gifts and events, here are a few suggestions from our 1997 special fin-de-siecle catalogue.

SUPER GIFTS

For him

Incompetent teacher badge. Big gold badge with '15,000 Club' prominently picked out in red. He may wonder what it all means, but you will know it refers to the estimate that there are 15,000 incompetent teachers. Leave it in the pigeon hole of any smartass who fancies himself. Guaranteed gales of laughter in the most jaded staffroom. (Ofsted Executive Toys, £6.99).

The Woodenheads. A wonderful collection of beautifully carved painted wooden heads to help keep his room tidy. The 'Lay Inspector' model is hollow, so he can keep all his bits and bobs in it. The 'Doesn't Give a Monkey's' has a projecting felt tongue, handy for pins and needles. The ever popular 'Big Woody' has two raised fingers, useful for keeping spare key rings. Its eyes light up and it burps when you press it. (Ofsted Executive Toys, £12.99 each, 'Big Woody' with velcro hair £19.99).

For her

Acronym kit. Crochet a personalised hat for a quango, exam board, fake qualification, or trendy new teaching method. Supplied complete with material, iron-on alphabet of letters and list of silly suggestions. Even beginners can soon learn to crochet a hat for a friend, with an acronym in capital letters on it to show imaginary affiliation, like World Association of National Kwality Assessors (WANKA), or Bachelor of Underwater Metalwork (BUM). Hours of harmless fun. (Bureaucratic Bull Plc, £14.99).

101

Multi-purpose abacus. Versatile present with a hundred coloured balls on rails. Endless possibilities. She can use it to log in her pupils as class sizes reach record levels, or for teaching maths. As an added bonus it offers lots of conversation pieces at parties, ranging from 'I'm a traditionalist', to 'My job involves a lot of balls'. (Good Ole Days Gems, £24.99).

For the kids
De luxe target set. Complete with bullseyes, bows and arrows with rubber suckers. When asked if your class has met Government targets, you will be able to say, in all honesty, 'They always hit their targets', and no-one will be any the wiser. If you turn up at staff meetings with an arrow stuck to your forehead, you can always pass it off as your own eccentricity, rather than poor discipline. (Millennium Enterprises Inc, £19.99).

COMPUTER SOFTWARE AND GAMES
Hitlist. A wonderful new suite of software for head teachers. Each member of staff is put on the database, complete with penalty factor scores on twenty different criteria. These include 'unco-operative staff governor' (10 penalty points), 'goes off sick when carpet being delivered at home' (15 points), 'union rep' (20 points), 'awkward bugger' (30 points). The program automatically computes an overall 'Dismissability Score' for every teacher and prints names out in descending order of redundancy. Saves hours of anguish. (Utterbastard Software Ltd, £89.99, free bottle of strychnine included).

Paperchase. A spectacular new CD ROM game with stunning graphics. The chase is set in the Palace of Bumf. Players start in the cellar with a few sheets of A4. The winner is the first person to tick a thousand boxes and reach the Chamber of the Brain-dead. Hazards en route include having to get past little gremlins, called NVQs, armed with dangerous weapons like 'range statements', performance indicators' and 'flufficued dingle-dongles'. Guaranteed to turn the most lively competitor into a cabbage. (Bureaucratic Bull Plc, £29.99)

CHRISTMAS LOTTERY WINNERS
The special Christmas awards to schools from the Lottery Fund have now been announced. The following schools have been given grants.

Lord Farnes-Barnes Academy for the Well-to-do
A grant for sports fields, 10,000 seater stadium, astroturf all-weather pitch, squash courts, gymnasium and Olympic swimming pool. £50,000,000

Gasworks Comprehensive
Contribution to bus fares for pupils unable to hitch hike to the Lord Farnes-Barnes Academy stadium (provided the Academy agrees to let snotty-nosed little erks in). £7.50

Poshville Preparatory School Staff Association
Suite of jacuzzis, teachers' bar and social club, helicopter, landing pad, fleet of staff limousines. £10,000,000

Swineshire County Primary School Staff Association
Dartboard, set of coffee mugs (seconds), pack of cards, new jockstrap for PE teacher, jar of Prozac. £16.99

FOUR NEW CAROLS TO SING AT THIS YEAR'S CHRISTMAS SHOW
All things bright and beautiful,
All creatures great and small,
All things wise and wonderful,
League tables kill them all.
The holly and the ivy,
When they are both full grown,
Will be chopped down when the school becomes
A light industrial zone.
Hark the Herald Angels sing,
That the post bad news will bring.
Now the head retirement seeks,
Ofsted's coming in three weeks.
See amid the Winter's snow,
Water leaks on those below.
Soon the governors get involved,
Sack a teacher, problem solved.

12 December 1997

Calculators may be used off the bone

There are heroes, superheroes and Desperate Dan. In a year where every week seemed to bring a new development, I thought the threat that Desperate Dan might disappear from the *Dandy* marked the lowest point.

When he was reinstated it was a defining moment for the century, proof that good guys can survive, even when the odds are stacked against them. Part of our collective childhood would have disappeared with him.

Desperate Dan was never all that desperate. Whatever ills befell him, he was always there for a fresh adventure the following week. If even the indestructible Dan had fallen, what bastion would have been safe in our society?

The year was full of threats of oblivion. The much admired Teletubbies came under fire, yet by the end of the year they had broken all records for toy sales and won an international prize for being 'educational'. In the 21st century they will be seen by the next generation of adults as one of the great memories of childhood. A seemly dignity will be restored to them.

Calculators too came under fire and were threatened with a ban. I have a very simple view of calculators, and of bans, for that matter. Prohibition is a strategy that should be used sparingly. It reminded me of when schools used to frown on parents for teaching children capital letters. What were they supposed to do? Pretend they didn't exist? Cover up all the shop signs, notices warning of DANGER, car number plates?

I have to use fiendishly complicated statistics in my own research. It would be hopelessly time consuming if I did not have a computer. However, I have always made sure that I can apply even multivariate methods, like factor analysis, by hand, so that I understand what is going on.

Calculators are an everyday fact of life. They are to be found in most homes. Walk into any branch of W H Smith or numerous other High Street shops and there they are. The solution is quite simple. The evidence shows that very little use of calculators is made in the infant school, so it is not, in any case, a problem at that stage.

Children should not use a calculator until they are competent in written and mental arithmetic, are absolutely secure in the manual solution of maths problems, and no longer make silly place value errors. Secondly, they should learn how to use calculators judiciously, once they are ready for them, so that they don't one day misuse them at home and in work. Thirdly, there must be separate 'calculator maths' testing, to check if they can use them intelligently and accurately.

Finally, if people are really anxious about the whole issue of modern information technology in the classroom, we should require schools to employ a man bearing a red flag to walk in front of any child using a calculator.

In a year full of symbolic events the use of target-setting for the year 2000 and beyond became a hot issue. Personally I cannot get worked up about the millennium. Sad and boring, I know, but for me January 1st in the year 2000 is merely the day after December 31st 1999 and the day before January 2nd 2000.

I am more concerned about what goes on in schools every day, than I am about some arbitrary date which would have no significance at all if we had a duodecimal instead of a decimal system. The problem about staking everything on targets of a certain kind for a certain date is that it can skew people's efforts. Individual dates come and go, but the enduring issues of preparing children for the rigours of the future are there every minute of every day.

My own memorable symbolic event in 1997 was an interesting one. I never go to do-it-yourself shops, as I am a firm believer in do-it-someone-else. However, one Saturday in the summer I went to a well known DIY superstore to buy a bath panel. Unfortunately it didn't fit, so I had to take it back. This simple event gave me a new insight into what counts as 'management' nowadays.

The woman on the checkout was very efficient, filling in the appropriate document and explaining what was involved. Then she rang her little bell, saying that she was not empowered to approve even a straightforward refund as it had to be counter-signed by 'the management'.

Intrigued at what kind of super-manager was employed to handle such high level policy matters as refunding a few pounds on returned goods, I looked across the vast store as we waited for 'the management' to appear. Would it be a whole team of besuited executives? A female power dresser? A bespectacled serious looking chap with briefcase, bowler and pinstripe?

In the event it was none of these. To my utter disappointment and astonishment 'the management' in question was a spotty youth in apron who lurched up uncouthly, bawling something like 'Wharra yer want?' to the middle-aged intelligent check-out.

I felt like muttering the words of an American friend who was once being pestered by an acne-ridden street salesman – 'Go and play under the traffic, kid'. It was sad to realise that it is not only in education that bright imaginative people are sometimes subject to the rule of the twerp.

All of which serves to remind us that optimism for the future must be an essential counter to the dreary in modern life. Let us hope 1998 will see sanity return.

Desperate Dan will live on, though he will never get a job in 'management'. Calculators will not be banned, better to get children to use them sensibly. Cow pie will be restored to school dinner menus. And fairies will dance at the bottom of your garden.

Happy New Year.

26 December 1997

Chapter 3
Ring in the New?

What's that in newspeak?

In exclusive private schools in New York children are no longer flops in the classroom. Parents who have paid huge fees are understandably upset when their offspring are given grade F for 'fail', so a number of schools have decided to abolish the category altogether.

Apparently the F graders of the wealthy are now being given marks like NS (needs strengthening) and NGA (not grade-appropriate). One school has even adopted the label RT (requires teaching), which I suppose must apply to every human being on this globe. Whether this little charade fools the parents, or the pupils themselves, is not known.

It is a common approach to problems nowadays. If something is unpalatable, never mind the reason, simply change the image. If you want to improve the image, then alter the language by substituting a novel and high sounding phrase to cover up the awful reality.

History is littered with well-intended euphemistic labels which in turn became offensive. What could be more positive sounding than 'Approved Schools'? The word 'approve' is a term of appreciation and commendation. Yet these institutions for the badly behaved eventually reacted against the very name that was meant to dignify them.

Some hospitals call their morgue 'Rose Cottage' to avoid any association with people being dead – or presumably, in more politically correct form, NB (needs burying) or NLRT (no longer requires teaching). I suppose it is preferable to be transported to what sounds like an idyllic rural retreat, than be carted off to the 'corpsorium' or 'slab lab'.

Political correctness on its own is often comical. The reason for this lies in its very detachment from action. Everyone knows that to substitute a new label for an old one is not a cure. It is often a cheap device aimed at hoodwinking people into thinking that action has taken place when none has.

The current fashion of preferring image over substance should end before it does any further harm. Nothing is gained by the mere dry cleaning of labels. It is like removing a 'Polluted beach' sign and replacing it with one that says 'Visitors are advised not to bathe in this water', instead of cleaning up the sewage. Given a choice I would prefer the more direct 'Swim here if you like vomiting'.

The trouble with the 'find a euphemism' solution to difficulties in education, therefore, is that it has a short shelf life when the root causes of the problems are not addressed as a top priority. If the climate in a school is wrong anyway, then before long just as much insult will attach to being labelled NS, NGA or RT, as there was to being called 'thick' in the playground.

The sole justification for euphemism is if there really is no feasible solution, and the unpalatable must therefore be made as inoffensive sounding as possible. Only then would a mere change of name be defensible.

So perhaps we should investigate extending the use of euphemism in schools. I am tempted to set up my own company, dedicated to dry cleaning unfortunate labels in education. We at BILGE (British Institute of Language for Gentrifying Education) will be working hard to eradicate politically incorrect terminology.

No longer will there be any 'incompetent' teachers. No sir. BILGE officials will be working hard to assist those who are CRAP (clearly require additional practice) or TRIPE (transplant radically improves professional expertise).

Pupils will not be labelled 'badly behaved' or 'delinquent'. These somewhat patronising and old-fashioned terms will be outlawed in favour of the more caring 'lad/lass inclined to transmit less educational sophistication or determination' (LITTLESOD).

At the end of the week teachers will no longer feel 'stressed'. This word has now become greatly overused and is in any case too dramatic a statement of the minor irritations that occur in any job, so we are excising it. In future the new politically correct term will be that a teacher is 'professionally incapacitated, starts thinking of funny farm' (PISTOFF).

Parents and governors who complain must not be spoken of in derogatory language. The cleansing department at BILGE will ensure that only approved labels are ever employed in staff rooms. Parents and governors with complaints will be in one of two categories, namely PAIN (presents adverse information nicely), or MENACE (makes excessive noise about children's education).

While we're on with it, we at BILGE may consider diversifying into other branches of the language cleansing business. One phrase I should like to see the back of is 'zero tolerance'. Its origin was in the obliteration of crime. Fair enough in that context, but it should not be used in education. It sounds smug and smartass and, like other catchphrases, it could one day explode in the face of its users.

'Performance indicators' is another one for the chop. Teachers and pupils are not circus chimps, nor are they calibrated along their edges. We are exploring possible alternatives, such as MUPPET (monitoring useful proficiency pointers in education and training).

At the risk of offending my many accountant friends, (well, the one or two accountants I actually know – oh, all right then, the bald headed bloke in glasses who once cornered me at a party), I have to say that the term 'cost effective' has run its course. It was handy for looking at inanimate objects, but became a deadly phrase in the human domain.

In the callous money mad world in which we live it would not be regarded as 'cost effective' to give extra help to children with special needs, rather than boost the able bodied and improve one's league table standing. The only answer is to find a more acceptable label.

The BILGE thought police have come up with a politically correct alternative term for attitudes towards money. In future, therefore, instead of 'cost effective' substitute 'be upbeat, give generous extra resources in teaching', or BUGGERIT in newspeak.

9 January 1998

Funny business this profit motive

Should private companies be allowed to make a profit from supplying classroom education to children? Should a consortium of schools be run by a business which, quite legitimately, is dedicated to earning as much money as possible?

We are not talking here about the sale of goods and services to schools by private companies, or the many excellent education and business partnerships which exist. It is rather the proposal that schools themselves can be run for a profit, with national pay agreements for teachers suspended.

I have to declare that I am totally open minded about the possibility of private businesses making profits from running schools. What do I care if some gang of spivs rips off education, or Flybynight Plc shareholders loot the public purse?

If voracious city sharks manage to filch scarce cash from the very pockets of the needy, carve a fast buck out of some hard up downtown school riddled with social problems, take the money and run, then good luck to them. Totally neutral on the issue, that's me.

Do not believe the hokum about how successful such privatisation has been elsewhere. Alongside any real or imagined 'successes' should be put many failures and scandals. Some of these took place a few years ago, in the United States, when there was a vogue for what was known as 'performance contracting', which involved private businesses being paid to teach children to read.

The same arguments were put forward in favour of 'performance contracting' that we hear now: that public provision was failing, business was better and more efficient, the profit motive guaranteed success, the free market would ensure high quality as the inefficient operators went bust.

Many contractors became so desperate for success they stopped at nothing. Handed lucrative contracts, awarded on

110

the promise that they would teach children to read more effectively than did their regular teachers, some simply coached pupils for the tests. In a number of cases they were so incompetent even that did not work.

No doubt a few of the entrepreneurs who are eager to lick clean the British version of the big jar of jam, will put forward the argument that 'efficiency gains' will produce the profits. Ha jolly ha, is the answer to that. What is euphemistically called 'efficiency' is often a staffing reduction, a service cut, or both.

It is hard to nail someone down to the detail of a contract when it concerns human matters, rather than inert goods. If a dealer who has been asked to supply 50 textbooks only sends 25, no problem. Just wave the contract and ask for the missing copies. Try protesting to shareholders if class sizes go up, or a special needs teacher is sacked.

So much hype is put into the positive benefits of business running education nowadays, it would be easy to forget the down side. Public service is on the whole altruistic and open ended. Professional people do what they feel is needed. Hence the voluntary extra-curricular activities that teachers have run over the years. Private businesses will not usually go beyond the contract.

Remember the poor railway passenger, stuck on a station one evening, gasping for a drink, who tried to buy a cup of tea from a passing vendor. 'Sorry, mate', was the reply. 'I've only got the concession for selling on trains. People waiting on platforms have to use the buffet'. The buffet was shut.

However, I don't want to be accused of not being progressive (Oops! Wash my mouth out with soap and water for even using the word), so I have been trying to imagine whether commercial and educational values can be reconciled, as the head teacher reports to the board of directors of the company running the school ...

'Ah, come in Jenkins, I think you know my fellow directors'.

'Er, yes, Mr Fastbuck. It's still a little bit difficult for me to get used to Fastbuck Funeral Services running Swinesville Comprehensive School'.

'No matter. Now let's look at the balance sheet. I see the Art department lost us a few thousand pounds last month'.

'Yes, I'm very sorry about that, but the gas kiln in the pottery broke, and we had to get a new one'.

'A new gas kiln. Now listen here, Jenkins, we could have fired a few pots for £50 an hour in the Fastbuck Funeral Services crematorium furnace, if you'd only asked. You've got to make full use of the Fastbuck business expertise and plant. Any of your lads misbehaving and we can take them away in one of the hearses for £5 a mile'.

'I'll try and remember Mr Fastbuck'.

'Now what's this about the head of Science wanting an additional salary award. How old is he?

'He's 63 next birthday'.

'Well he's not got much bargaining power then. Offer him half his present salary, and if the shock is too much for him, we'll do him a half price funeral with a nice oak casket. What the directors want to know, Jenkins, is what are you going to do about the Art department deficit?'

'I've been working on that, Mr Fastbuck, and I thought we might hold a jumble sale'.

'A jumble sale?'

'You know, the parents bring things in and we sell them one Saturday morning'.

'So what expenditure would be involved in purchasing these goods, what's the profit margin, and what are the labour costs?'

'No, it's not like the funeral business, Mr Fastbuck. People give us things they don't need any more, and then parents man the jumble sale stalls for free'.

'I'm sorry Jenkins, I don't understand the words 'give' and 'free' here. You mean, there are no purchase, transport or labour costs, so there is a hundred per cent profit margin? Really? So tell me more about these parents who work for no salary. Can any of them handle a shovel?'

23 January 1998

Carry on busking

A few years ago, in teacher training, when tutors could not think what written work to set their trainees, they would turn to an old favourite. Write an essay on 'The changing role of the primary teacher'.

It was a safe bet, because the role was, in any case, always changing. If for some reason it wasn't, then the tutor could easily pretend that it was. 'You mean, you hadn't thought about the primary teacher as social worker, Miss Scattergood? Tut tut.'

Coping with many exacting roles has now become part of the daily art and craft of teaching. No-one can be unaware of the weekly calls for teachers to be tougher, meet the challenges of the 21st century, satisfy growing demands from parents, help Britain compete internationally, compensate for poor home backgrounds.

Even the traditional role of teacher as transmitter of knowledge has undergone several changes in the last decade. Since the advent of the national curriculum primary teachers have had to be a cross between Brain of Britain and supreme champion of Mastermind.

'Please miss, where's the Indus valley?', 'How do microorganisms break down waste?', 'Why doesn't plastic go rusty?' 'How do you work out the probability of winning the lottery?' It is a far cry from tadpoles and sticky buds.

Design and technology has really stretched teachers' subject knowledge. Our research at Exeter has consistently shown it to be the subject about which people feel least confident. If you followed the national curriculum literally you would only teach one subject a week – technology. When small children had finished designing, selecting materials, making objects, evaluating and improving them, there would be no time left for anything else.

The first occasion I taught national curriculum technology, I asked the deputy head in the school if there was anything I ought to know. 'Yes', she replied, 'In this authority you're not allowed, in infant schools, to use scissors that cut'. Thanks.

As a keen cook, I always felt it was a pity that cookery became part of technology. I remember talking to one of the gurus of the national curriculum in technology. 'It's all-embracing', he enthused, 'so you can do business studies as well. For example, you can design, make, and then market a beefburger'.

This was bad news to someone like me who loved cooking and saw it as an art not a business. 'Design a beefburger'. How about a round one? 'Select materials'. Beef perhaps? 'Make, evaluate and market it'. Er, I don't think the public will really go for cork table mats enriched with the contents of Darren Rowbottom's nose.

If the teacher-as-polymath role has changed, so has the teacher-as-scavenger role. Primary teachers have always been adept at looting society's detritus and getting children to mould it into cheap art. I remember sending in Vim containers when my children were young and getting them back painted purple with rice crispies glued to them, and labelled 'Star Ship Enterprise', or 'Kevin Keegan', I couldn't really tell which.

Scavenging is still a valued talent, only now teachers say, 'If you've got any CD Roms you're throwing away, bring them in to school'. And that neatly brings in another developing role, namely teacher as information technology expert. Primary teachers who a few years ago got a nose bleed when they switched on their BBC model A, are now expected to be wizards of the spreadsheet and expert surfers of the Internet.

Times have certainly changed. I remember going to a village primary school in the mid 1980s, where a couple of old dames told me they were absolutely thrilled. That nice Mr Baker had given them a brand new computer. Really? How exciting. I enquired innocently what they were they using for. Oh, they weren't actually using it at all, one old dear replied. They hadn't dared to unpack it.

Two roles have not changed in the slightest, however. The detail may be different, but the roles remains the same. The first is teacher-as-busker. The ability to think on your feet, get out of scrapes, cope with the unexpected, is as challenging as it ever was.

I once presented a live Radio 4 series with seasoned broadcaster Eric Robson. Each programme lasted one and a half hours. Before the start the producer would explain that week's disasters – lack of link-up with remote studio, broken radio microphone, poor acoustics, or whatever. 'Never mind', Eric would say reassuringly, 'we'll busk it'.

The second unchanging role is that of personal relationships expert. Primary teachers have usually been renowned for positive relationships inside and outside the classroom. If these ever go amiss, the consequences can be drastic.

As we buskers love to sing:

Two lovely black eyes.
Oh what a surprise.
Only for telling a man he was wrong.
Two lovely black eyes.

23 January 1998

Titans' clash forces debate into corners

This is the big one. It's the last showdown. It's Tyson v Holy-field. It's Godzilla v King Kong. It's the World Cup final. It's High Noon. It's ...

Sorry about that. I get carried away with the sporting hype on television, as each football game is personalised: 'Alex Ferguson's megastars take on Big Ron's rejuvenated Owls'. Utter rubbish, I know, but I fall for it, until the brain-corroding tedium of the actual game.

So I have been looking at the Chris Woodhead (Ofsted Rovers) versus Tim Brighouse (Birmingham United) press accounts of the Office for Standards in Education report on Birmingham local education authority.

I was very interested in this inspection, as I chaired the Birmingham education commission in 1993. We delivered a damning report on the LEA, and several recommendations on matters like baseline testing and target setting later became national policy.

Fortunately for Birmingham Tim Brighouse was then appointed Chief Education Officer. He visited hundreds of schools, infusing massive energy into improving classroom practice and the life chances of the city's children.

In 1998 Birmingham gets a brilliant Ofsted report, describing it as 'a success story', performing better than any LEA inspected. The report offers perfectly fair criticisms and many helpful pointers about such matters as improving school attendance.

So why the fuss? The answer lies in the sentences that seem to have accreted while passing through the central Ofsted sausage machine.

I wonder what the Ofsted drafting process would have done to Shakespeare. 'The quality of mercy is not strain'd, it is generally sound', or 'This was the noblest Roman of them all, but he didn't use approved Ofsted teaching methods'.

There are isolated remarks like: 'The LEA might, for example, valuably ask itself how the use it makes of Ofsted inspection data, important as that is, can be squared with the CEO's public views about the need to reform Ofsted'. Oo, naughty Tim, slapped hands. But what on earth has this got to do with the rest of the report and the quality of Birmingham schools and LEA?

These detached asides clarify the agenda. Tim Brighouse is criticised for his 'rhetoric'. In classical times 'rhetoric' meant the art of skilful speaking or writing, and wealthy Athenians paid Protagoras 10,000 drachmas to teach it to their sons. Here 'rhetoric' is used pejoratively, mentioned four times in the same paragraph, alongside 'sound-bite', used twice.

A Sunday newspaper article last Summer quoted Ofsted 'sources' as saying that the inspection of Birmingham would show there was a lot of hype, and that was before a single inspector had set foot in the city.

So what has Tim Brighouse said and done that led to this clash of ideologies? The report says that Birmingham celebrates success, but should be more public about failure, though it acknowledges the LEA has taken firm action on failure. Since Woodhead's public rubbishing of teachers has only offended them, give me Brighouse's approach every time.

The second ideological spat is over teaching methods. Tim Brighouse encourages teachers to choose strategies in the light of evidence and context. Ofsted believes teachers should be directed more on how to teach.

Ofsted, you see, has discovered interactive whole class teaching, i.e. standing before the class asking questions. All right, stop laughing. I know people have been doing that for years, but don't spoil the excitement of discovery. As I tell myself each time seven year olds get excited about magnets, 'It may be the hundredth time for you, but it's the first time for them'.

I have studied classrooms for over 25 years, noting down events, studying individual pupils, interviewing people, testing achievement, reading research literature. Nowhere can I find the philosopher's stone, the single teaching method that turns all to gold.

They found it in the nineteenth century. Training institutions were called 'normal schools'. There was a single norm which every teacher was filed to fit. That was why Dickens said of M'Choakumchild that he and 140 other schoolmasters 'had been lately turned at the same time in the same factory, on the same principles, like so many pianoforte legs'.

Poor old Confucius. He wrote in his Analects, 'If ... I have dealt thoroughly with one corner and the pupils cannot then find the other three for themselves, then I do not explain any more'. Little did he realise that Ofsted would one day redis- cover the nineteenth century and consign him and thousands of other thinkers and practitioners to the dustbin of history.

Let there be no ambiguity. If teachers in future are told how to teach by Ofsted, and presumably inspected accordingly, then it is the death of teaching as a profession. It will still be a job, but not one for those with imagination or spirit. Throw all your information technology on the skip for a start. Welcome back M'Choakumchild.

If you doubt this will happen, consider the success of the Ofsted rhetoric, and the determination with which it is being hyped among the powerful. A recent Times leader stated: 'Some LEAs still espouse eclectic teaching methods that have been shown to be far less effective than those recommended by Ofsted, the inspectorate'. Goodbye choice.

Despite Birmingham's excellent report, this clash of ideo- logies, sadly, polarises an argument that should be flexible. In the end Brighouse versus Woodhead becomes the wider stage: spirited, imaginative Miss Scattergood versus Gradgrind; Beethoven's Ode to Joy versus the Dead March from Saul; a profession versus 'just a job'. In football terms, Brazil versus Poland.

Imagine the television commentary: 'Brighouse picks up the ball with silky skill. What a marvellous dummy as he ghosts samba-style round two Ofsted defenders. Only Woodhead, the Ofsted centre back, to beat now, and ... Oh, I say, there's a nasty tussle in the goalmouth. That has to be a red card.' But which one will the ref send off? If it's Brighouse, then it's RIP teaching as a profession: died 1998.

6 February 1998

Give norm-crushers their head

A Creativity Committee. I like the sound of it. Provided nobody panics if it comes up with unusual suggestions, then setting up a national committee to look at the place of creativity in education will have been a good idea.

It will also be a means of reinforcing an important element of our national heritage, for we are, in general, a creative lot. Conformity is the characteristic valued in many education systems and those who step out of line are punished or humiliated. In Britain being different is not yet outlawed. While other nations are good at copying, we are brilliant at inventing.

It is not that every teacher welcomes creative ideas, but having a spark of originality has some chance of recognition and reinforcement in British education. 'That's Miss Snooks over there. She always comes to school with a bacon sandwich strapped to her head. But it's all right. She teaches art'.

The assumption that 'creativity' is only for art, music and English teachers is one of many misconception about it. There is a place for imagination and invention in all school subjects and activities. The curriculum should have several dimensions, as I pointed out in my book 'The Cubic Curriculum', and imagination is one of them.

'Creativity' and 'committee' are not words that are normally juxtaposed. 'Can we approve the minutes of the last meeting?'. 'I propose we sing the minutes of the last meeting, Mr Chairman. I've scored them for three part harmony and a small brass ensemble ...'

That is another misconception about creativity. It is often assumed to be random, shapeless, diffuse, rarefied, fragile. Sometimes it is. Equally, however, it can be deliberate, disciplined, sculpted, commonplace, robust – Acme Creative Ideas Inc (Office hours 9 a.m. to 5 p.m. weekdays). There is no reason why a committee cannot be imaginative, just because some are not.

The most exciting ideas from children can come in un-expected circumstances. I was impressed by the best of American work on creativity a few years ago, and have often tried out the ideas with classes. Analysis of creative people's achievements had shown that those with original ideas often made a sideways leap into the unknown, unafraid of being ridiculed or challenging orthodoxy.

A series of strategies was developed to try to recreate this process for children. For example: think of a silly or unusual idea; try the exact opposite of what seems to be obvious; work on improving one part of your idea; look at related issues and see what ideas can be borrowed and adapted.

Encouraged to think the unthinkable, children have few adults' nervous inhibitions about producing dotty ideas. It is only as we grow older that we become terrified of novelty. What do you do when new teachers suggest an idea? Mutter 'How interesting', through clenched teeth, 'or at least it was when we did it in 1969'?

Yet artists and musicians, like Picasso and Schoenberg, were quite prepared to turn things on their head, and inventors often have to ride the ridicule of their fellows. Pioneers of heavier-than-air flying machines, stuck with the analogy of birds, designed gawky machines with cumbersome flapping wings. Eventually it was the crazy idea of having no wings at all (balloons and rockets), or immobile wings, that actually worked.

I was once using structured brainstorming ideas with a primary class, trying to improve the motor transport. They came up with suggestions like 'have a jet of air instead of a windscreen' and 'make cars travel up motorways coupled together like train carriages'.

One girl seemed hesitant. 'Put the engine in the door', she ventured, expecting laughter. Children do laugh during brainstorming, but often out of the excitement. 'No, put the engine in the wheel', she went on, 'put an engine in each wheel'. Later I read that Detroit automobile engineers were experimenting with the same idea.

If we want children to be truly creative we must be prepared to live with the discomfort of both the process and the outcome. How would you have reacted to the following true event, had it happened to you?

The class was asked to paint a picture of someone's head. Most children produced the usual postage stamp stereotype, head-and-shoulders portrait. One boy, however, covered his paper with a variety of red, yellow, brown and grey daubs and streaks.

'What is this supposed to be?', the teacher asked in bewilderment at the colourful melange, 'I asked you to paint a picture of a head'. 'I did', the lad replied, 'but I just wondered what someone's head might look like from the inside'. Many teachers would show it approvingly to their colleagues, but niggling unease is not far away.

We once did a research project at a school for young offenders, using a creativity test which involved a toy elephant. The toy was placed at the front of this class of tough boys who had been in trouble with the police. They had to write what they would do to the toy 'to make it more fun to play with'.

One lad produced a single response and then laid down his pen. He had simply written: 'Put a bomb up its bum and blow up the whole bloody school'. The answer was not in the test manual, so it was certainly 'original', as many anti-social norm-crushing ideas are, but 'creative' would have been a cruel misnomer.

While we angst over British children's sometimes cavalier attitude to exactitude in spelling or number, the Japanese see 'individualism', a close relative of creativity, as a desirable 21st century aspiration. We already have a fair bit of it, and I hope the new Creativity Committee will help preserve and enhance it. But are we fully prepared to live with the challenging consequences of youthful originality and novelty, exciting though these may be?

20 February 1998

The bogeyman who won't shut up

Forgive me while I finish putting on my costume and make-up. Now where's that thick black cloak? Ah, there it is. And where did I put my big black broad-brimmed hat? I had it only a minute ago when I was sticking the spirit gum on my curly black moustache. Yes, got it, next to the heavy black boots. Right, I'll just slip on my boots and sinister mask and then I'll be ready to go out and frighten a few people.

Sorry to keep you, only I have been reading the newspaper accounts of Chris Woodhead's annual rant, I mean lecture, to which, for some reason, I was not invited. Apparently Woodhead attacked schools in general, and three professors of education, Robin Alexander, John MacBeath and myself, in particular, as being responsible for the poor quality of garden gnomes.

No, wait a minute, let me just check what he actually said. Ah yes: 'the real heart of darkness, by which I mean the trivialisation of culture and the erosion of belief in the intellect which has destroyed the life chances of so many children.' I say, steady on, Wooders old son. Have you been skim reading Matthew Arnold again?

Matthew Arnold was a schools inspector, so perhaps Woodhead sees him as a role model. The irony is that, in 'Culture and Anarchy', Arnold attacked the 'Philistines' in Victorian society for lacking 'sweetness and light', as good a description of the Office for Standards in Education as you could find. He was a very human inspector too, no advocate of the Gradgrind philosophy that Ofsted espouses nowadays.

Anyway, Prince of Darkness, Phantom of the Opera, that's me: the sinister Victorian figure looming out of the midnight mist, who skulks around trivialising culture and eroding belief in the intellect. So I thought I might as well dress up for it.

Woodhead implies that I want to replace subject disciplines in the curriculum. No I don't, as he would know had he read my book 'The Cubic Curriculum' properly. School subjects are actually the first dimension of the curriculum model that I put forward. There is a whole section on the importance of subject knowledge.

Anticipating that some idiot might distort the model, I even wrote in the preface: 'I hope no-one will do mischief to it. For example, I am at pains to point out that subject matter is very important and this is not diminished by taking a look at other aspects of the curriculum ... No doubt some skim reader will ignore these warnings'. Unfortunately, some skim reader did.

Robin Alexander is also misrepresented. 'Does Robin Alexander really believe that any individual will be empowered in the 21st century if he or she has not learnt to read?', Woodhead asks.

No he doesn't believe reading is unimportant, nor did he ever suggest such a loony idea. What is more, I have never met a single person on the entire planet who believes this, largely because anyone who did would probably have been locked safely away.

The annual lecture is worth close inspection, for it had a curious mishmash of an agenda. The bizarre title of the talk was 'Blood on the Tracks'. 'Blood', for goodness' sake? What is going on here?

Woodhead began by pointing out that it was his fourth annual lecture, saying: 'Who knows? If David Frost works his habitual alchemy on the Prime Minister we might soon be heading towards double figures'.

I assume this is a little joke. It surely cannot be an attempt to bounce the Prime Minister into renewing his contract for another five years when it comes up for review in the autumn, given that it was on the Frost Programme that he originally said Woodhead's job would be safe after the election.

Is it pure chance that two of the people misrepresented, Robin Alexander and myself, are attacked as members of the board of the Qualifications and Curriculum Authority? According to Woodhead, the next national curriculum must 'conform to the curricular emphasis and pedagogy of the literacy and numeracy strategies', i.e. teachers must not only be told what to teach, but how to teach it.

He wouldn't be trying to dragoon the QCA board into sharing his nostalgia for a Victorian 'back-to-basics' curriculum, would he? Well he is wasting his arrows on me. There are numerous ways of constructing a curriculum and I prefer to listen to the many intelligent points of view that people can offer, rather than submit to the first and loudest noise.

But let me end on a helpful note. The right-wing tabloids love Woodhead's rants. So here are *Ten Facts You Never Knew About Professors Of Education*. They:

- rattle your television aerial so that snow spoils your favourite programme
- stand in front of you in the bank, paying in £100 in 1p and 2p coins
- phone during a meal to offer a camping holiday in Salford if you buy double glazing
- knock your glass over in the pub
- cause volcanic eruptions like the one in Montserrat
- widen the hole in the ozone layer
- blast the ball high over the crossbar during the 'sudden death' penalty shoot-out
- park too close to your front and back bumpers (that's usually Robin Alexander and me, working as a twosome)
- seal up the little hole in the tops of salt pots in cafes
- alter the Birmingham Ofsted report (only kidding, we don't do that)

Anyway, I'm just off to trivialise a bit more culture. From time to time I shall put on my Prince of Darkness outfit and leap out suddenly on Woodhead, crying, 'Look out! There's a professor of education on the loose. Run for your life. Here comes the bogey man. Whooooooooo!!'

It may not stop him on his irrevocable path towards ruling the entire universe, but bugger it. He won't shut me up.

6 March 1998

Love is a nod, a grunt and your own chair

How can you know whether you are doing a good job, or if you are a potential Advanced Skills Teacher? Do crowds of pupils queue up at the end of every class, saying, 'Thank you once more miss/sir, for another truly inspirational lesson'?

Does the head slip a couple of used tenners into your hand as you cross the playground, muttering, 'Genius, pure genius'? If this is the case, then I have two questions: what planet are you on, and are the tablets working yet?

Teachers are in the same category as parents cooking a meal. As someone who is keen on cooking, I have learned over the years that if your children don't throw the food at you, or say 'What the hell is this muck?', then it is probably an excellent meal. Just don't expect any praise.

In universities nowadays we actually have to compile 'esteem indicators'. Pathetic, I know, but that is the sorry state to which higher education has been reduced. In the desperate quest for kwality, lecturers have to fill in forms, ticking esteem indicator boxes with headings, like 'medals, prizes'. Conference addresses, mentions by fellow academics, invitations to lecture, all are recorded under numerous headings.

It is hilarious to think of some distinguished scientist earnestly entering the digit '2' in the 'medals, prizes' box, with not enough space to explain that these are, respectively, a Tufty Club road safety bronze medal and a Nobel Prize. Before long academics will parade through town with a placard saying, 'Please Love Me, I need the ratings'.

The possibilities for finding evidence of esteem are endless, from 'They all wept with emotion when I finished my lecture', to 'Professor Splutzenheimer of Kleinpiddel University mentioned me in his seminal article 'The semiotics of the 17th century antemasque' (*Kleinpiddel Gazette*, volume 23, pages 34-35)'.

Teaching has always been a job where it is hard to tell whether you are genuinely esteemed. For most people teaching is a bustling activity, with a thousand or more interactions in a single day. There is no leisure time for standing back and admiring yourself at work.

In these hectic circumstances it is easy to delude oneself, for good or ill. I have often observed lessons and kept a record of which children are answering questions. When teachers are then asked to estimate roughly how many children responded to questions, some will say, 'Oh, most of them, I suppose – was it twenty-odd?'

Sometimes the answer is six or seven, but because these pupils are especially eager to reply, and often seat themselves centrally when given a choice, the impression is that everyone has joined in. It is simple for me to look out for such matters as an observer, but far more difficult to see them clearly when I am teaching.

The same problems occur when seeking evidence of esteem. Some teachers may overestimate their effect, but many are hard on themselves, believing that they are achieving little. Appreciation emerges in small increments, a smile or a nod maybe, rather than a spectacular explosion of gratitude. With adolescent boys, a raised eyebrow or a monosyllabic grunt is the nearest they will come to ecstasy.

Given the masochistic nature of teaching and the tendency that some practitioners have to flagellate themselves, perhaps we should ask people to look out for 'contempt indicators' instead of evidence of esteem. There are endless possibilities here: 'Head teacher stubbed cigarette out on back of my hand', or 'Inspector was excessively polite when he said my teaching was 'generally sound''.

Esteem is often subtle and understated. One of my former students was once told by a class at the end of her first term, 'You're the first teacher we've had who's lasted a whole term'. It was their equivalent of giving her an Olympic gold medal.

Praise can sometimes occur in perverse form, the opposite of what seems to be signalled. A new teacher was concerned that some of the class seemed to have taken a dislike to him, so he had a confidential word with one of the more streetwise pupils. 'Perhaps a few of the kids do dislike you a bit', the lad announced, 'but you've got to remember they absolutely hate all the other teachers'.

In order to satisfy the thirst for a set of indicators of teachers' standing, I have compiled my own authoritative scale of 'esteem indicators' for potential Advanced Skills Teachers, the Definitive Underpinning of Pedagogical Esteem. I fully expect DUPE to become a standard instrument in future. It teases out the most subtle, nay perverse, evidence of being valued for what you do.

Pupils gave me an apple (extra point if no cyanide can be seen dribbling from stem).

Children have given me an affectionate nickname (no points allowed for 'Chalky' or 'Tinky Winky').

Head sent me a note saying I would be in the running for an Advanced Skills Teacher award (minus one point if it included the words 'when pigs can fly').

Parents give me presents (no points for packet of amphetamines, or gift with label saying, 'I hope Michael does well in the SATs').

Elected union rep at AGM (no points if it happened while you had nipped out to the toilet).

Governors named me 'best teacher of the month' (minus a point if it was for August).

Local authority selected me, out of all the staff, to go on a course (no points if it was entitled 'How to keep order').

Caretaker says my room is always the tidiest (no points if you teach Latin, extra point if you teach art, but check caretaker for irony first).

I received several cards on Valentine's day (no points for 'get well soon' or 'deepest sympathy' cards).

Colleagues always let me have a comfortable chair to myself in the staff room (check armpits before awarding point).

20 March 1998

A mantra does not a lesson make

'Fifteen-fifteen-twenty-ten'. Does this mean anything to you? The chorus line of a rugby song? The dates of some obscure dynasty? An advertising jingle? If you are a primary teacher, it could soon be your daily mantra.

Fifteen-fifteen-twenty-ten is the 'official' Department for Education and Employment structure of the literacy hour. There will be fifteen minutes of whole class 'shared text', fifteen minutes of whole class 'focused word or sentence work', twenty minutes of 'group and independent work', and ten minutes of whole class revision. Fifteen-fifteen-twenty-ten.

This will operate day in, day out; week in, week out; month after month; year upon year; from reception class to the end of Year 6; seven years in all, or 1,260 daily slices of fifteen-fifteen-twenty-ten. And that is just the literacy hour. When the numeracy hour does a similar thing, primary children will have 2,520 predictable daily time shares. Pass the Prozac, Mabel.

It is all very well to say that these timings are 'approximate'. So what? Is fourteen-sixteen-nineteen-eleven' any better? It is the predictability of the macro-strategy and its insensitivity to the context that are the killers, not the exact length of the units.

The lesson starts with half an hour or so of whole class teaching, whether children are five or eleven, clever or slow, excited or bored, whether thirty minutes is too little or too much. The decision has been made in London.

Let us be clear what I am objecting to. I am in favour of giving a high profile to literacy and numeracy. I like the idea of literacy and numeracy hours. I personally love phonics, giving children structure and the means of attacking new and un-familiar words. I love phonics (I repeat this, in case some idiot who skim reads this article says I do not, even though I have taught phonics for thirty years and included it in a reading scheme I wrote).

I am objecting to two things: (1) the suggestion that the fifteen-fifteen-twenty-ten literacy hour structure is compulsory, when it is not; (2) the bogus claims that have been made about non-existent international research evidence.

Tony Blair expressed my sentiments very clearly when he made a major speech on education at Didcot Girls' School in June 1996. He said: 'It is not of course up to central government to prescribe classroom organisation in 25,000 schools. Professional judgement according to local circumstances is important'. That, in a nutshell, is my first point.

Fifteen-fifteen-twenty-ten is in fact VOLUNTARY, but the impression being given in the press is that teachers must do it. Not true. I have culled the thesauruses and dictionaries of the world to find the most precise expression for the identical pattern of lesson plan being obligatory for all. The correct technical term is: 'Aaaaaaaaaaaaaaaaaaaaaargh!'

My second concern is that 'international research' is said to justify the fifteen-fifteen-twenty-ten pattern and what goes in it. No it doesn't. There is no interplanetary or intergalactic evidence either, unless I have missed some Neptunian journal article, or Alpha Centauri monograph.

In the Leverhulme Primary Improvement Project, which I directed, we did find certain common features among the expert teachers we studied. They equipped children with autonomy, celebrated success, set high standards, matched books to individual interests, but they had many different individual ways of expressing these features.

We never saw one teacher using the fifteen-fifteen-twenty-ten split, or indeed any identical macro-strategy, day in day out. I should be grateful for details of firm research evidence, (as opposed to travellers' tales and flights of the imagination), for everyone singing in unison. One reference will do.

To satisfy this desire for compulsory uniformity, perhaps the big toe of every primary teacher in the land could be wired up to some London-based electronic factory hooter.

Booop! All start the first fifteen minutes. Booop! Now switch to the next quarter hour. Booop! Time for twenty minutes of group work. Booop! Fetch your brain back from the fridge and see if the children are still awake, or indeed present. Booop! Now it's time for the art hour. Booop! First fifteen minutes: painting by numbers.

Some claim that having a compulsory national straitjacket will cut planning time. No it won't. It needs more effort to flog the same dead horse into life every day. Nor will it save teachers from reinventing the wheel.

The phrase 'reinventing the wheel' is often overdone, but here it is a good analogy. The diagrams of the literacy hour are wheel-shaped. Like the wheel, however, the literacy hour should be capable of taking infinite forms. Wheels can be big or small, thick or thin, spoked or unspoked, tyred or tyreless.

Moreover, stick too rigidly to the wheel and you will never invent the ship, the helicopter, or the hovercraft. Swear solely by buttons, and there will be no zips, ribbons, hooks, or velcro. If doctors had been too committed to the leech, they would never have discovered penicillin, developed the vaccine that eradicated smallpox, perfected transplants, created artificial hip joints.

You've got heart disease? No problem. Fifteen minutes with a leech on your bum, fifteen minutes with it off again, twenty minutes to swallow three tadpoles and a newt, ten minutes to be sick. Fifteen-fifteen-twenty-ten. International research has proved it. Works every time, squire.

Fifteen men on a dead man's chest. Yo ho ho ... oops! Sorry, but the mantra is beginning to addle my brain. Fifteen-fifteen-twenty-ten, that's it.

I would be lost without wheels. But the wheel goes round and round and round and round until it wears out. Fifteen-fifteen-twenty-ten. Fifteen-fifteen-twenty-ten. That is the twelfth time I have mentioned it. Only another 2,508 to go and primary education will be over.

I love the wheel. I just don't want to be one.

3 April 1998

Seize the day ... and the money

Never look a gift horse in the mouth. No, let me rephrase that. If someone actually gives you a horse, and few people do nowadays, take but a quick look in its mouth. If it is actually breathing, accept it with alacrity. You can always sell it for a few quid down at the knacker's yard. Every little helps.

I was a bit surprised at the moans when all schools were given their £1,000 books bonus. 'This will create enormous problems for us', said Ned Nock (59), chairman of Swineshire County Primary School governors. Come on, Ned, you might win the lottery one day: 'Oh dearie dearie me. What am I going to do with all these millions. There's Aunty Mavis wanting to go to Blackpool for a start ...'

Time was certainly short, and in a perfect world, maybe, there would be several months to prepare, but in the considerably imperfect one that we currently inhabit, most things have to be done by yesterday, so I prefer to act first and moan later. Knowing how to busk it may turn out to be the key skill in the fast moving world of the next millennium.

Teachers have always had to be opportunistic scavengers. Seizing the moment is an important part of professional expertise. There was a cartoon of a few years ago that showed two children sitting together in class. One was whispering to the other, 'Don't look out of the window or she'll make you write a poem about it'.

I once visited a primary school where this cartoon was almost a reality. Right next to one teacher's classroom a building site opened up, as some entrepreneur decided to build a crescent of detached houses. Rather than surrender to the daily banging, clanging and assorted renditions of the current top twenty, she decided to turn adversity into triumph, so she took her eight year olds round the site, accompanied by the foreman.

Bricks were measured, details of house construction were noted, the supply of electricity and water was investigated. The crowning glory was a magnificent wall in the classroom, constructed entirely from empty shoe boxes she had begged from a local shoe shop, all neatly painted brick red. It was a fine example of living maths, language, geography, and technology.

Not being thrown by the unexpected is vital to teachers, but it is a characteristic that will also be of value to children in their adult lives. Who can know what the future will hold? They may unexpectedly be made redundant, have to learn new skills, move to another town, or indeed take up residence in a different country.

In these circumstances the ability to cope with novelty, to respond speedily and positively in strange situations, may be a life saver. Employers increasingly seek people who are adaptable and flexible, able to use their initiative. In work or in the family, people have to react quickly to the unpredicted.

It is the permanent worry of each generation that the next one will be incapable, paralysed by its own incompetence. Whereas we could light a fire with a magnifying glass and a small torch, we like to believe, cook a nourishing casserole from a discarded boot and an Oxo, or crochet a bungalow from a pair of old socks, this lot would starve to death if the supermarkets shut for a day.

Yet resourcefulness and survival can be learned. They are not just rare traits that only a few lucky people have at birth. Thousands of adults believe that they are at the mercy of mysterious external forces, that there is nothing they can do with any cruel cards they are dealt by life's mischief.

Teachers and parents are important role models here. If they appear to be easily flummoxed, tending to fret and wring their hands, rather than act decisively, children will learn by example that indecision is the norm. They might decide, early in their lives, that almost every problem is insoluble, to be addressed by others, not themselves. It is a recipe for a nation of passengers, with few drivers.

That is why I was worried at the occasional negative reaction to the government's £1,000 book offer. I hope that any future bounties will be seized. Don't ask too many questions. If it is tainted you can always give it back later (less a handling charge, of course). Take the money and run like hell, is my advice.

Then, once you are round the corner, get your breath back, count the loot, bank it and make sure you spend it before anyone changes their mind. 'You want your fifty grand back? Sorry squire, you'll have to knock those inside toilets down and sell off the bricks and fittings'.

The government has promised to make money available for school buildings, so being prepared is vital. If the phone rings, sound positive and dynamic, no ifs or maybes. Appear to be right on top of it, raring to go, and have a copy of *Yellow Pages* handy. It may soon become the most important book in education.

Talk in an upbeat voice, giving the impression that you are prepared to have a go at anything and, most important of all, don't hesitate, even for a second. Just keep saying, over and over again, the key word in these circumstances: 'Yes ... yes ... yes'.

Ring ring. 'Is that Swineshire Comprehensive?'

'Yes. We've got an estimate and it's £1,497,296'.

'But I ...'

'Yes. Scroggins and Scroggins have agreed to be the architects, and Buggins Builders have put in the best tender'.

'But I only ...'

'Yes. They can start on Tuesday and be finished by the end of term'.

'But I only rang to say that our John's got a bad cold, so is it all right if he misses PE?'

17 April 1998

Please don't beam me over

You have to hand it to the right wingers, when it comes to producing ripping ideas. Now they want private companies to be able to make a profit out of running state schools.

Since 80% or more of schools' budgets goes on salaries, the only significant profits will come from getting rid of teachers. Switching off lights and using envelopes twice would produce peanuts.

The latest wheeze for private companies to make a profit out of state schools is new technology. One teacher could teach three classes, it is argued, by appearing on screen before them. What planet are these people actually on?

This was exactly the argument put forward when radio was first tried out in schools in the 1920s. It was said that one of these 'wire-less boxes' could be put in every classroom, saving a fortune in salaries. How typical of the right wing to express nostalgia for the failed ideas of yesteryear.

I have done several video link-ups myself, but I am glad that I am used to presenting on radio and television. Sitting alone, at the mercy of a temperamental technology, no audience to bounce off, is weird. You talk to a blank wall, while looking out of the corner of your eye at a monitor with a tiny image of a group of people in a room miles away.

For the uninitiated, the use of video links is always eventful and goes something like this, if the telephone lines are actually working.

'Welcome to the video conference, ladies and gentlemen. We have contributors in America and Australia, so it's certainly worldwide communication. Let me bring in Dr Larry Barry, head of the Fastbuck Distance Learning Centre at Dimesville University. Larry, are you there?'

Close-up of the back of someone's head. Muffled sound of technicians on both sides of the Atlantic muttering about ISDN

6 not being compatible with ISDN 2. Beep beep. Back of head becomes front of head. Broad smile, moving lips, no sound.

'Larry, I'm afraid we can't hear you. Can someone do the sound? That's better.'

'... finest distance learning programmes in the United States ... beep, crackle ... thousands of students ... crackle ... superb communication network ...'

Caption appears saying 'Dr Barry Larry, head of program'. ' ... if you look at this map here ...'

'Larry, er Barry, we can't see the map. Barry, the map ... we can't actually see it.'

'Crackle, beep ... Incidentally, I love Scotland, and it's so good to speak to you folks in Scotland.'

'We're in Stoke, Barry, that's in England. Look, we'll come back later. Let's switch to Professor Clueless in Adelaide. Professor, are you there?'

Keystone cop figure crosses screen jerkily, carrying wires and plug. Close-up of Professor Clueless's bald patch as he bends down to pick up his light pen. Professor faces camera with nervous smile of someone caught picking his nose.

'Hello, beep beep, is that Stockport, England?'

'It's Stoke actually, Professor. Tell us about your distance learning programme. Is it a success, and what do you actually do?'

'crackle crackle ... the three key concepts, the three Ds as we call them. I'll just put this graphic up That's 'distance' and 'delivery', crackle ...'

Out of focus graphic appears upside down, then disappears again. Audience now in hysterics.

'We can't see the graphic, and we didn't get the third D, Professor, what was it again?'

'Dollars, Stockport. It's the most important of the three'.

Even if the technology of projecting a talking head and supporting graphics to remote locations becomes 100% foolproof, I cannot see that Year 4 or Year 9 will sit quietly, watching the screen and learning assiduously.

Perhaps the intention is to have an ex-army type in each room to keep order. 'Right you 'orrible lot. Sit up straight and listen to the Captain, er I mean teacher.'

Retired sergeant-majors would probably come cheaper than teachers and you could have classes of a hundred. This would then be the final fulfilment of the right wingers' dream to re-create the 19th century in its entirety, and also make tidy profits for the private companies.

Like the Professor said – dollars, Stockport. That's what it's all about.

1 May 1998

And for our next trick ...

'What can I expect in the interview?'. Whenever trainee teachers ask me that question, I reply, 'Almost anything'. Interviews follow no single pattern of questioning. After seeing many of them, I am unshockable.

The first important point to remember about going for an interview is that there is no break. Some candidates forget that they are under scrutiny from the moment they arrive. 'I don't reckon much to the blond woman', a school secretary once said to the head, 'she was so rude when she came in'. The secretary was highly esteemed, so one boat was comprehensively incinerated, even before the conducted tour.

A few years ago it was not uncommon for interviewees to spend barely an afternoon in a school: an hour or so to look round and twenty to thirty minutes with the head teacher. Nowadays that perfunctory version of selection is a rarity.

A whole day is commonplace and applicants may be asked to teach a class, or address the staff or governors. Some schools spend two days. The interviewing panel is usually a sub-committee of the school's governing body, so it will have lay people, like parents or local business representatives, as well as educational professionals on it.

While being shown round, one candidate confided that he would beat the British all-comers' sprint record down the drive at 4-01 each day. An Oscar-winning performance in the actual interview achieved nothing. The head had already asked escorting teachers what they thought of the applicants and relayed this to the selection committee.

Each year there are always rumours about real or imagined student teachers who have skilfully arranged a string of interviews at attractive seaside resorts along the south coast, just failing to get each one and so enjoying an extended tour of the English Riviera while their colleagues sweat away completing their teaching practice.

Since schools may not pay your travel expenses if you turn a job offer down, make sure your lottery ticket has come up before embarking light-heartedly on a trip to Carlisle or Truro. However, if you reject an offer because the conditions are not as advertised, for example, because the school has changed the year groups to be taught, then they should pay up, since you have acted in good faith.

The mixture of lay and professional people on an interviewing panel can lead to interesting questions, from the obvious to the unexpected. 'What car do you drive?', one set of candidates was asked by a chairman of governors, enraged by a Renault covered in Greenpeace and Save the Whale stickers. It turned out it was the art teacher's car.

One local authority used to insist on interviews for pool appointments being conducted by the whole of the education committee. Each councillor was given a particular question to ask. Candidates came out telling those waiting outside that the 'Why do you want to teach in Swineshire?' bloke was sitting third row up, fourth from the left.

Parent governors in particular may pose the plonkingly obvious question. Sensible applicants take each question seriously, rather than patronise one person or another. 'Do you like children?' may be asked in all sincerity by a parent aggrieved that one of her children's present teachers clearly does not. To reply, 'Is the pope a catholic?' demeans both questioner and questioned.

One problem that many interviewees face is whether to put on an act or be themselves. The only advice worth giving is: 'Be yourself'. That way you can sleep at night. If you act out some imaginary person, then you will kick yourself for being so foolish when you don't get the job, or you will be successful and have to let people down or live a lie.

There is a very common question which is guaranteed to flummox at least one candidate. It is the very obvious: 'If you were offered the post, would you accept it?'. I was present on one occasion when, to everyone's embarrassment, the applicant actually leapt up exclaiming, 'Oh thank you very much'. Sit down, sunshine, it's only hypothetical.

The reason for the question, often put towards the end of the interview, is clear. The panel will eventually have to weigh up the merits of different people. Some may have decided the post is not for them, so a great deal of time could be wasted on telephone calls and correspondence. It is much easier to eliminate the disaffected and concentrate on those who want the job. Be prepared, and reply either 'yes', 'no' (with reasons, if possible), or 'I'd like a little time to think about it'.

Another hazard is the chairman who debriefs unsuccessful candidates afterwards and makes a pig's ear of it. 'Your trouble was the bad reference from your tutor', one dipstick explained, prior to quoting extensively from a confidential reference. Distant noises off of tutor and student locked in combat.

Let nothing throw you. Some rum people get on to interviewing committees, so dotty events do occur. A head once asked all applicants for a languages post to sing a song in French. He believed music was an important motivator. Perhaps Pavarotti got the job.

A chairman of governors stared people up and down as they came in, because she preferred tall people. The staff looked like a basketball team. Do not be surprised either if the school appears to be in complete chaos. One head started asking questions about geography teaching until the head of department reminded him it was a maths post.

My favourite shambles story occurred when I had acted as referee for a student. The girls' school concerned made a monumental bog-up and sent the 'unsuccessful candidate' letter to referees as well. On receiving the missive telling me I had been unsuccessful in my application for the post of German mistress, I could not resist writing back saying how upset I was, even though I had never applied. I received an apology addressed to 'Professor Wargg'. You just can't get the staff nowadays.

1 May 1998

Dalek dogma is a bitter pill

A prescription is what you get when you are ill. It should not be applied to all teachers in all circumstances. Current attempts to prescribe how teachers should teach, however well intended, are mistaken.

In addition to the prescriptions for literacy and numeracy, there are proposals for national schemes of work for the other seven subjects of the primary curriculum. 'Unprecedented Government intervention in almost every lesson', as the *Daily Telegraph* reported it.

I welcome voluntary schemes. Any teacher can learn from other people, or from videos of classroom practice. Only the arrogant believe they know it all.

In 'Education: an alternative vision', produced by fifteen academics in 1993, I wrote: 'There should be a huge emphasis on literacy right at the centre of the infant school curriculum'. So I applaud the government's campaign on literacy. It is only the prescription I dislike.

Asking teachers to split each hour into the same 15-15-20-10 minute formula, for every class, day after day, is like telling journalists that all articles must have fifteen sentences setting the scene, fifteen developing the story, twenty sentences giving two opposing points of view with quotations, and ten sentences of summary. No choice of structure, whatever the story.

I am not here addressing the extreme views of Chris Woodhead. In a *TES* article in April he said it was 'dangerous' for teachers to work out their own best professional practice. Striking a match in a gas-filled room, treading on a tiger's toe, that's what I call dangerous. Working out best practice is what professional people are paid for.

In his annual lecture he asked whether we wanted reflective practitioners or people who could teach reading, as if thinking about the job was somehow in opposition to doing it. Woodhead's own vacuous utterances are so intellectually woolly that debating with him is like arguing with a bobble hat.

I want to persuade people whose opinions and motivation I respect, like Michael Barber and John Stannard, director of the national literacy strategy. Michael Barber (TES, May 1) offers the names of researchers on whose findings the strategy is based. This is not the issue. I am in favour of using research in this way. Many of my own books on class management, questioning and explaining are based on research, but not with compulsion.

In any case, research on reading, even in the references that Michael Barber quotes, is not sufficiently clear cut to justify wholesale adoption of fixed strategies by all. Experimental groups 'beat' control groups by relatively slight amounts. No method trounces the rest. The context – pupil age, background, interest, teacher expectation – is very important.

I have asked for a reference to research demonstrating that all teachers should sing in unison, irrespective of context. None has been produced, because none exists. Where is the evidence for two thirds of the time being devoted to whole class teaching, whether pupils are bored out of their skulls, or so engaged they want 100% of it? There is none.

Compelling all teachers to use 'traditional' methods, assumes this has some incontrovertible virtue. What other professions look only to the past. Where are the traditional dentists (no anaesthetics, big forceps), traditional plumbers (earth closets are best), traditional journalists (quill pen and pony express), traditional engineers (wooden structures that catch fire)?

In the nineteenth century teachers taught huge classes. There were few books, illustrations; no videos, computers or interactive technology. Little choice existed compared with today's many possibilities.

A head who had attended literacy training summed it up: 'There were some very interesting ideas from the literacy people, stressing flexibility, but then this prat from Ofsted [not Woodhead] came in and made it sound all rigid and compulsory'.

THE PRINCE OF DARKNESS

The nineteenth century ended with the demise of a bad policy. Payment by results was finally abolished in 1898. What a pity, exactly a hundred years later, if we exit the twentieth century with another policy that, in retrospect, will seem just as wrong.

How many teachers, recalled by the famous in the 'You never forget a good teacher' campaign, used the identical lesson structure with every class, every day? Not one. Daleks teaching by prescription cannot meet the huge demands of the next century.

15 May 1998

Could do better ...

In 1967 the Plowden Report proposed annual reports for parents, but not until the 1990s did they get a legal right to have one. The era of 'satisfactory work and progress' spawned the idea, but the computer age eventually delivered it.

I watched with fascination over the years as 'satisfactory' gave way to the repeated naming of children in school reports, in order to make it all seem personal: 'Fiona writes nicely in Fiona's book, does Fiona; and Fiona's sums are nicely done – by Fiona, of course ...'. Well done, er, what's her name again?

Hitler's teacher commented on his poor powers of leadership. Nowadays he would probably have written, 'Adolf needs to improve his social competence and interpersonal relationships, as he scored at a low percentile in the school's PSME programme'. No doubt Mr Hitler Senior would soon have been knocking on the door, saying 'You what?'.

Writer's cramp is not the only hazard lying in wait for the unwary report writer. Simple though it may seem on the surface, report writing is a bear trap. To criticise a child is to criticise a gene. The wrath of the whole family will descend on the perpetrator.

One of the reasons why multiple choice items became so popular in the United States was that, when parents objected to teachers' subjective judgments, it seemed easier to quote scores from supposedly objective tests: 'You don't agree with Michael's grade? Here's the scoring grid. Check it yourself'.

One new teacher was determined to pull no punches in his written comments, believing that parents needed to know the truth, not be given some sterilised version of it. Phrases like 'A cruel misuser of the English language' adorned his class's reports. He was lynched at his first parents' meeting.

The sheer volume of prose involved when writing individual appraisals of thirty or more children, often about several different subjects, soon led to computer power being drafted in to help. Commercial firms were eager to sell their user-friendly software, guaranteed to give parents the impression that every comment had been lovingly crafted by hand.

Typically you have to select from choices and the computer prints them into a template. The personalised sounding 'I am delighted to say that your Fiona has performed well in English this year ...' is likely to have been generated from: 'I am (insert adjective) to say that your (insert name) has performed (insert adverb) in (insert subject) this year ...'.

I wonder what would happen if the program went seriously amiss. 'I am delirious to say that your Fatso has performed stupendously well in advanced skiving this year ...'.

School reports have made steady progress over the decades, you could say. With some room for improvement, of course.

Try to make the report sound personal, so that it really is about Fiona and not Thingummy or 'this class'.

Be specific where possible. 'Slipshod homework' is too vague. 'Needs to check his maths calculations carefully before handing them in' is more focused.

Avoid technical jargon. 'She has covered all the key stage attainment targets and flangified breezlebugs of the globberific noodledoms' means less than 'She has grasped all the topics we have covered in science, apart from electricity'.

Make positive comments, indicating good points, so that criticisms are put in context: 'His written work is usually good, but the presentation of it is sometimes untidy', rather than 'Scruffy presentation spoils the look of his written work'.

Never scribble the words 'illegible handwriting'. It is embarrassing to have to decipher them for someone.

Check for spelling errors and always use a dictionary when in doubt. Mangled words like 'standerd' and 'sentance', or the incorrect use of the apostrophe, soon wreck credibility with parents and pupils.

Try to be kind and stress the positive without over-enthusing about every single aspect of every pupil's work. A diplomatic, but accurate and fair-minded account is needed. Save gushing for oil wells.

Discuss the report with parents whenever possible. Text can be very dry. At the next parents' meeting refer back to your comments and check subsequent progress.

Remember human judgments, however well researched and intended, can sometimes be frail, so never give the impression in a report that the last word has been spoken. There is always hope for the future.

Before putting pen to paper, imagine you are a parent receiving the report. What will it mean? Empathising with the audience is just as important for teachers as for children learning to write.

22 May 1998

Wallop the teacher, 50p a go

According to a recent opinion poll the reason why children thought they did badly at school was because of their teachers. It was another front-page story.

One day I must glue together the full picture of all these negatives about the profession. There have been so many different criticisms, it is easy to lose track of what the villains are up to now.

Over the years teachers have been accused by Marxists of preparing children solely for life in the factory. The bell at the end of each lesson was merely a preparation for the factory hooter, it was said. Future workers were being taught blind obedience.

Meanwhile, the right wing was attacking schools for not being interested in the world of work and for allowing children to do what they wanted. Future workers were being taught blind disobedience, it was claimed. Capitalist lackeys or wild anarchists, which is it? Both, apparently.

Another line of attack is that school is too boring because teachers simply peddle facts at children. Marking books in red is naughty. Creative potential becomes smothered under all this transmission, indoctrination and recrimination.

But teachers are accused by other critics of not transmitting the culture, of neglecting to correct children's work, of stressing creativity not substance. Hello schizophrenia.

When national tests were first introduced in the early 1990s, government ministers of the day said that this would rumble teachers. Schools' assessments would be over-generous, it was predicted, to cover up deficiencies, but the national test scores would be lower, thus exposing teachers' inadequacies.

When the first national tests were eventually marked, the scores were actually higher than teachers' assessments. So did education ministers rush to apologise, or confess that they had been wrong. Quite the reverse. They said to parents that teachers were underestimating their children's talents. It was a nice example of having your cake and also ramming it into someone's face.

Too strict, too lax? Too rigid, too flexible? Too many facts, not enough facts? Stick-in-the-mud, or trendy progressive? Hatchet-faced assessor and jailer, or laid back hippy? Up and down. Round and round. Left wing in, right wing out; right wing in, left wing out. In out, in out, shake it all about. You do the hokey-cokey and you turn around. That's what it's all about. Hey!

In the Prater, the huge funfair in Vienna, there used to be a sideshow called the 'Watschenmann', a 'Watschen' being the Austrian dialect word for a clout across the face. It consisted of a large dummy with a padded head. You inserted your money and then walloped the plastic face. A meter indicated how well you had done.

It used to cost two Austrian schillings for five seconds of pure therapy. I often wondered which teacher had posed for it, or indeed whether one was still inside, collecting the wrath of the world against those who had tried to teach them. Perhaps it will become a fundraiser in Britain, when schools have open days. Only 50p to smack the crap out of the deputy head.

There are so many opinion surveys, critiques, reports, it is probably easier to say what teachers are not guilty of causing. So far as I know, but don't hold your breath, no survey has yet shown that teachers caused the hole in the ozone layer, or any plague of locusts, Nor has the teaching profession been proved to have started mad cow disease. Suffered from it, yes, but not caused it.

After much thought I believe I can explain how these contrasting criticisms have come about. There are, in fact, only two teachers who have caused all the mayhem and negative publicity, though they have taught in many schools. They are called Denzil and Albert.

Denzil is a fierce disciplinarian, Albert is a raver. Denzil underlines everything in red, Albert automatically puts 'good' at the bottom of any piece of work, even if someone, when asked to write an essay entitled 'What I did on my holidays', hands in a single thumbprint in the middle of an otherwise blank sheet of paper.

While the other 439,998 British teachers just get on with their job, Denzil and Albert do the hokey-cokey. They have a lot to answer for.

29 May 1998

Bite your nails? That's nothing

In an uncertain world, where no-one's job is safe, there is one sure way of making people feel jittery. Ask them about their health.

'How are you feeling today?'.

'Fine, absolutely fine, yes fine, never felt better, really fine, brilliant, fine, just fine'.

If you ever have to announce that there might be a few redundancies, don't even think of saying to anyone, 'You're looking a bit pale'. Intensive care patients immediately leap off life support machines and pole vault through brick walls.

It was no surprise, therefore, to read that some teachers reacted negatively when sent a health questionnaire containing items like, 'Do you bite your nails?' and 'When was your last period?'. Paranoia is fuelled, as people wonder what will be done with their answers. Fantasy soon takes over.

Will there be a knock at the door one night? 'Good evening, Mr Buggins, health police here. Sorry to trouble you, but I gather it's some time since you last had a period...'.

Or does some hawk aggregate all the responses?

'Now look here, Simkins, do you realise that 63.7% of Swineshire teachers are biting their nails, especially on Mondays. You're in charge of health. What are you going to do about it man?'.

'I've tried, Mr Ramsbottom, goodness knows, I've tried'.

Health and other kinds of personal or private questions have been taboo ever since we were tiny. Early socialisation soon teaches us that there are some things that you simply don't dare to ask.

'Don't ask Auntie Edna about the big wart on the end of her nose'. 'Auntie Edna, what's that big lump on the waaarhg abxxxxb yerrr ... '. Muffled sound of four year old being carted off upstairs with parent's right fist in throat.

When faced with questions we have been trained since birth to be discreet about, most of us have no idea how to respond. Some people reply in an aggressive manner, often protesting innocently that they are only doing what was required. Children do this to teachers when they print out half a CD Rom and then say, 'But Miss, you did ask us to give you a full answer'.

This concept, in the field of management, is known as 'malicious compliance'. It is what happens when people do exactly as they are told, but make sure that their boss suffers as a result.

'I want everything sent by e-mail'.

'Right, sunshine, I'll just e-mail you a few telephone directories to read'.

The cousin of this strategy, when respondents nervously send up the whole exercise, might be called 'facetious compliance'.

'Do you bite your nails?'.

'Not since I came off the heroin'.

'How long is your willy?'.

'About four foot ten, but his sister Helen in Year 9 is five foot six'.

I suppose the most irksome aspect of health questions and other queries thought to be intrusive, is the mystery that surrounds them. Why does anybody want to know if I bite my nails? Is there a conclusive socio-medical article in an obscure journal somewhere proving that teachers who bite their nails are less effective than those who have immaculately manicured mitts?

Moreover, why do some of the questions seem so irrelevant to the job? The real health test is whether someone can actually survive in the school and classroom. I could understand items on a questionnaire better if they were more sharply focused, like:

1   Do you smell?

2   Do you bet school funds on the horses?

3   Do you break wind in the middle of assembly?

4   Do you lurch round your classroom, dressed as Napoleon, shouting out 'The end of the world is nigh', while sniggering incessantly?

5   When the deputy head comes into the staffroom looking for someone to cover for an absent teacher, do you cry out, 'I've got Lassa fever'?

6   Do you deliberately go cross-eyed when faced with an angry parent?

7   Do you spend the first ten minutes of every lesson coughing and saying, 'Where's me fag?'?

8   Can you feign a limp when asked to take a PE lesson?

9   Does marking books give you indigestion?

10 Are you constipated even during an Ofsted inspection?

Biting your nails sounds so harmless.

12 June 1998

Are you listening, bankers?

Teachers and banking have always gone together about as well as strawberry jam and cold cod. This is partly because the modest salary awarded to teachers is of little excitement to bankers. No money, no esteem. It is also because the two jobs are polar opposites.

Teachers have little money at home or in school, bank managers have oodles of it. Schools are often crumbling, banks are luxuriant. Public versus private, principles versus profit, elbow patch versus three piece suit.

The tension between bankers and pedagogues was confirmed by the unhappy experiences of a teacher who applied for a credit card with a building society. He was told he had ticked the wrong box on his application form.

Eighteen year old students are offered a Donald Duck watch to open an account, but teachers are not even categorised as 'professional' in this building society. They have to tick the box headed 'other'. He wrote back and told the toffee noses where to put their strip of plastic.

It reminded me of when I first started teaching and wanted to borrow £100 to buy a ten year old Austin. The bank manager looked me up and down contemptuously, as only true snobs can, and said, 'We don't lend money to teachers'.

I felt like replying, 'Well we don't teach the children of dickheads', but did not, because it would have been undignified and untrue. The temptation to wipe one's nose on the velvet curtains, however, was overwhelming.

On another occasion, having drifted all of £10 into the red for three months in a row, I was invited to meet his deputy manager 'to discuss your financial options', as he put it. The deputy was a perfect clone of the chief prat.

'I think it's clear what the problem is', the number 2 sage began. I perked up at the thought of having my funds sorted at a stroke. 'We are living beyond our means', he went on. We? You might be, sunshine, I thought to myself, but I'm just plain skint.

Teachers ought to be an attractive proposition to a bank: salaried, straight, sober, law-abiding citizens. What more could anybody want? What banks would prefer, in a nutshell, is someone who earns a lot more loot.

Whereas schools are expected to be consistent in their policies and practice, banks can veer wildly from one year to the next. Some time after my bank manager refused to lend me £100, banks changed their policies completely. Suddenly it was good to borrow and be in debt.

Each visit to the bank saw my snobby friend transformed. Now he oiled around the counters, sidling up to unsuspecting customers: 'Pssst. Want a washing machine or a new colour television?' I felt like dialling 999: 'Get me the police. There's a maniac on the loose trying to ram tenners into people's pockets'.

Nowadays I meet some very pleasant bank managers, particularly those who are school governors, but these early experiences when you start teaching can leave deep scars. Unable to cope with the hypocrisy of banks, I have rarely been into one for twenty years. When they ran the advertising slogan 'there's a bank manager in every cupboard', I kept my wardrobe locked, hoping mine would suffocate.

Perhaps the answer is to pretend to be better off than you are: 'Oh yes, in my job I am responsible for an eight figure budget' (£29.50 for books, £21.99 for equipment); or 'You will recall that my friend Mr Major, when he was Prime Minister, said he wanted every teacher to have a new car standing in his drive' (but it was a Dinky car and you ran over it in your 1983 Skoda).

Your own finances could also offer useful source material and real life data for the numeracy hour, particularly effective for teaching the normally difficult concept of 'negative numbers'.

Alternatively, try being assertive. If the bank manager turns unpleasant, threaten to take your account elsewhere. He will then get it in the neck for losing a customer.

How do you take a deficit to another bank? Nothing could be easier. You simply go in and say, 'Give me £100, I want to open an overdraft'.

26 June 1998

How to tackle the little sods

Pupils who misbehave in school are often described in the research literature as 'deviants'. The word suggests that most children follow a straight path of acceptable behaviour, but some decide to make a detour via anarchy.

The evidence supports this view. The great majority of children in both primary and secondary schools are indeed well behaved. My own research, like that of others, has shown noisy chatter, not gross misconduct, to be the most common form of misbehaviour. Schools are generally places where order is to be found. You are safer walking the corridors of a school than the streets of a city.

The politically correct term for naughtiness nowadays is 'manifesting more challenging behaviour', but nuts to political correctness. 'Being a little sod' is often more honest.

I came across my own version of 'challenging behaviour' recently when refereeing some five-a-side football matches for 12 and 13 year secondary pupils. Refereeing school football can be hazardous. I once had to send off a parent.

One team only needed a draw to qualify for the next round, so they deliberately wasted time on throw-ins. The score was 0–0 with seconds left. I did my teacher/referee bit, telling them to get on with play and I would be adding extra time for time-wasting.

Then it happened. An opponent burst through, drew back his foot to shoot and was hooked down from behind by a defender a few yards short of goal.

Loud blast on whistle. Foul. Direct free kick. Player picks himself up, places ball and scores. Full time only seconds later. Result 1–0. At this point the 13 year old losing team goalkeeper goes demented.

First he insists it should have been an indirect free kick. I explain. Indirect free kicks are for obstruction, not for kicking the lights out of an opponent who has gone past you, but kids never know the rules.

Next comes the 'he dived' ploy. Correct. It was that magnificent somersault with pike which people do when their legs are hacked while running at top speed.

More sullen griping and muttering. The lad cannot cope with losing, but his behaviour is the thousandth imitation of a thousand displays of petulance from adult role models who should know better. Deviance begets deviance.

Teachers vary in what they regard as misbehaviour, and in their response to it. Many different strategies are used to avoid or terminate deviance.

One teacher used to start the school year by taking off his jacket and then lifting a huge oak desk on to his shoulders before putting it down again. This is known as the 'Sumo', or 'double hernia' approach to class management, fine for retired wrestlers, not recommended for seven stone weaklings who get sand kicked in their face.

More subtle is the negotiated settlement, or 'Henry Kissinger'. Teacher and pupil are both happy with the outcome, because honour is satisfied all round. It is the technique I used with my daughter when she was two and yelled 'No!' to everything. 'You're not going to refuse to go to bed are you?' 'No!' 'Well clear off then'.

While some teachers try hard to understand each antisocial act (the 'St Francis of Assisi' strategy), behaviourists see everything in the light of Skinner's experiments on rodents, carefully reinforcing approved behaviour and ignoring whatever is disapproved.

This 'ratological' approach is sometimes accompanied by a reward system. Occasionally sweets are offered for good behaviour, presumably on the grounds that tooth decay is a fair swap for fidgeting. I have not found that ignoring bad behaviour necessarily leads to what behaviourists euphemistically call 'extinction'. Ignore profane language, for example, and it often gets worse.

So what did I do about the 'challenging behaviour' of the juvenile goalkeeper? I started with a St Francis ('It's a rotten feeling when you lose'), moved on to a quick bit of ratology ('You played well'), and, when that produced more abuse, ended with a Sumo ('Now look here, sunshine').

Later he returned and tried to persuade me that he had spotted a penalty incident which the rest of humanity had missed, a nicely attempted Kissinger. It only failed because I was in charge of the whistle.

10 July 1998

Teacher watch: a summer special

As schools break up for the summer, doctors are not preparing to cope with a rush of teachers suffering from withdrawal symptoms during August. Most teachers will be so keen to escape for a while, that few will need Prozac to tide them over until September.

If teachers are eager to go on holiday, however, that is as nothing compared with their pupils. For children holidays are magic. The thrill as a grown-up of driving through the Alps, or flying into an Italian airport, pales alongside the sheer excitement of seeing Blackpool Tower on the horizon as a child.

I remember childhood holidays as if they were yesterday. They began with packing the bucket and spade, as opposed to the mosquito repellent and sun lotion of today. Then we got on the train, since few of us had access to a car.

The most exciting part of the rail journey from Sheffield to Blackpool was crossing the Pennines through the Woodhead Tunnel, several minutes spent in darkness before we emerged. Nowadays the Woodhead Tunnel, or 'school inspection' as we like to call it, involves several weeks of darkness.

Finally the sight of the beach and the squawks of seagulls completed the magic. It is virtually impossible to recreate it in adult life.

One reason why teachers do not suffer from withdrawal symptoms during holidays is because many find it hard to switch off daily routines. If you see someone picking up litter and tut tutting about mess, it will either be the local loony or a teacher on vacation.

Watch out for the person organising an untidy fish and chip queue into a straight line. Ten to one it's a teacher. If she's saying, 'Now don't be silly', then it must be an infant teacher.

There are other giveaways for the eagle-eyed. See if you can spot the English teacher (inserting the missing 'm' in the word 'accommodation' on a notice), or the geography teacher (counts all the passengers twice on any bus excursion).

If anyone corrects your French and makes you repeat the phrase again (but this time with better intonation), it must be a modern languages teacher. The holidaymaker who splits each hour of the day into fifteen minutes of sunbathing, fifteen minutes for a drink, twenty minutes of quiet reading and ten minutes of table tennis, has just been on a literacy hour training course.

The anxious guest rushing round the hotel to find a substitute for the waiter who hasn't turned up is probably a deputy head back home. The one organising a local authority grant to improve the hotel swimming pool is almost certainly a head, as is the one smarming round any parents present.

I wonder if school inspectors fill in those evaluation questionnaires you get on aeroplanes and in hotels by writing 'generally sound' in each blank space.

Academics are the same. When bus couriers say, 'Good morning everybody. My name is Darren and we'll be taking you to the Acropolis', the smartass rabbiting on about 'a temple to Victory and the Propylaea started in 437 BC' is almost certainly a classics lecturer.

One of the hazards of being an academic on holiday is having a PhD. Airline staff always note anyone called 'Doctor' on the passenger list as a possible medic ('We've got two doctors on board').

When I got my doctorate I always dreaded having one day to explain that a PhD in classroom interaction process analysis was going to be of little help to some poor beggar having a coronary at 30,000 feet. ('Now sit up straight and stop making such a fuss about a silly little thing like a heart attack').

After a fortnight of being a teacher while on holiday, perhaps the logical consequence is to behave like a holidaymaker when teaching again in September.

People could return to school wearing a Hawaiian shirt, sing the 'birdie song' in assembly while strutting up and down clucking, put a towel down to reserve a favourite chair in the staffroom, pour a can of lager over anyone who misbehaves. According to some newspapers that is what happens in schools now, so there is nothing to lose.

Have a good summer.

24 July 1998